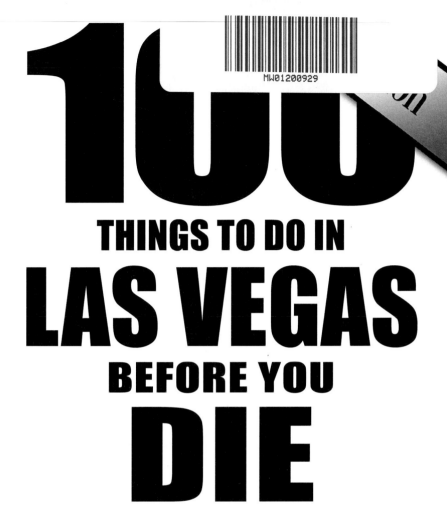

100

THINGS TO DO IN

LAS VEGAS

BEFORE YOU

DIE

Welcome to Fabulous Las Vegas Sign

2nd Edition

100
THINGS TO DO IN
LAS VEGAS
BEFORE YOU
DIE

• •

SHAUNDA NECOLE

REEDY PRESS

Library of Congress Control Number: 2024949025

ISBN: 9781681065649

Design by Jill Halpin

Cover photo courtesy of Shaunda Necole

Unless otherwise noted, all photos are courtesy of the author or believed to be in the public domain.

Printed in the United States of America
25 26 27 28 29   5 4 3 2 1

DEDICATION

The Las Vegas Strip is in a town in Nevada called Paradise. Destinations in Paradise have Las Vegas addresses, so even though people think they're in Las Vegas, they're actually in Paradise!

But really, what's the difference?

This book is dedicated to Tony, my soulmate in life and heartmate in Paradise. Thank you for sharing the dream of living in Las Vegas. Your constant encouragement to push boundaries and challenge the norm inspires me daily.

Seven Magic Mountains

CONTENTS

• •

Music and Entertainment

Sports and Recreation

Culture and History

• •

Shopping and Fashion

• •

ACKNOWLEDGMENTS

I want to thank all the local businesses and attractions in Las Vegas for inviting me to visit their unique venues and share their fascinating stories. The Neon Museum and CasaMadrid by Churros were among the first to respond, and their warm receptions left a lasting impression on me.

I'm grateful for my parents, Mary and Charles. You were the first to embrace and nurture my colorful artistry and free-spirited ways. Your support has been instrumental in my journey.

Thank you to all the English teachers who encouraged my creative writing, notably Mrs. Bach (sixth grade), Mrs. Makridakis (ninth grade), and Mrs. Bulman (11th grade).

To my kids, Destiny and Dahvian, thank you for letting me guide and lead by pursuing my dreams. I hit the jackpot with you two.

Thank you to everyone who has visited me in Vegas. I appreciate being your official tour guide and showing off this fantastic city.

I'm a Southern girl from coastal Virginia who, 15 years ago, had an outlandish dream of living in Las Vegas. Many people dream about it, but here I am doing it! I've made my mark in this well-established town by creating a unique and heart-centric business that contributes to the city I love and proudly call home. Thank you!

• •

PREFACE

There's the Vegas you think you know, and then there's this!

Las Vegas may be known as Sin City, but it also has a reputation as the city of high hopes and big dreams. Settled in 1905 as a railroad town, today Vegas is one of the top-five "dream cities" in the US. Still recognized as a casino town, it's sarcastically described as a place where people come together and hope for a miracle!

As a longtime Vegas traveler turned local, I'm excited to share the real Las Vegas that tourists rarely get to know—the sensational and showy, as well as the soulful and wholesome. Because it takes more than slot machines to keep tourists happy and ensure there's something here for everyone.

Vegas is also a neon dreamland where we love a party atmosphere in everything we do. (Spoiler alert: there's a disco bathroom here!) From first-class hotels and entertainment, world-renowned restaurants and shows, touring DJs, and star-studded residencies, Vegas offers unmatched luxury and much more to explore! UNLV professor and prolific author Hal Rothman once said, "No one thinks Las Vegas is real; it is an illusion, but visitors willingly suspend disbelief and pretend." This quote captures the essence of Las Vegas. The city thrives on creating larger-than-life experiences that often blur the line between reality and fantasy.

I come from a family of caterers, musicians, and entertainers, so naturally, I've always been drawn to Las Vegas. I'm just a tourist who fell in love with the city and now proudly calls Southern Nevada home. Yes, I am a local who enjoys visiting the famous Strip, even during busy sporting events and touristy holidays. That's because Vegas is a town that's a little wild in color and a lot free-spirited, something like me, a local with a tourist-like spirit and unmatched lived-in expertise.

This may surprise you, but Vegas locals do not live on the Las Vegas Strip! While rightfully world-famous for more than 100 reasons, the Strip is only half the story. So, this book is a passionate presentation of the best and most unique things to do in Las Vegas. It's a collection of my two decades of carefully curated experiences and best-kept secrets that many locals don't even know. I unveil the stories of iconic casinos, secret hotels, world-class entertainment, restaurants, shopping, and stunning natural attractions—with a bonus of my best Vegas travel tips and life hacks that'll make you feel like you won the jackpot!

An out-of-this-world Sphere Experience and panoramic Strip views on the High Roller. Or nature excursions like hiking Red Rock Canyon, visiting the quiet town of Blue Diamond, lounging by the shore at Boulder Beach, or indulging in fantasy-like Zen moments with gentle snow flurries inside the Fontainebleau's spa. There's no shortage of unforgettable experiences.

Tourism in Las Vegas is booming, with almost 300 hotels, more than 156,000 hotel rooms, and nearly 140 combined stadiums, showrooms, and arenas. The annual number of overnight stays in the city is always on the rise, with an occupancy rate of nearly 85 percent. More than 40 million people—and counting—visit annually, and close to 3 million have made this top-five US dream city their home.

· ·

Vegas is officially the most popular city to visit in America and is the most searched vacation destination online. Vegas is the destination, and the Strip is a vibe. If you've never been here, some folks describe visiting as taking your favorite place and turning it up to 11! At the same time, Vegas feels like casual West Coast energy where everything's shiny, new, and cool—except our summers, of course.

Yes, the West is the best. And in Vegas, we know how to win big! We're a city of firsts that pushes boundaries to limitless possibilities. The future of entertainment happens in Vegas first. This place is a vibrant universe hiding within its glittering facade as a mere city. The Entertainment Capital of the World is where the extraordinary becomes the norm, captivating visitors with its "Viva Las Vegas" innovative spirit.

The most recognized city in the Battle Born State of Nevada is a melting pot of diversity—musically, culturally, and in terms of sports and cuisine. Whether you're an early riser or a night owl, Vegas attractions are ready to entertain you whenever you're ready. And whether you like it or not, you'll have the time of your life in this magical, unrealistic city!

Let these 100 calls to action and adventure in this book guide your determination and intrigue for uncovering Las Vegas things to do—world-famous attractions, natural hidden gems, and tucked-away escapes only for the select few to find. Up and down the Strip and beyond, this diversity, vibrancy, and curiosity make Las Vegas a city ready to be reveled in, experienced, and explored.

Remember, you are the spirit of Las Vegas!

—Shaunda Necole

This book is designed to help you make the most of your time in this fabulous city.

Consider it a souvenir passport, and collect autographs from each featured business or attraction. If you're a local, use it as a boredom buster by opening the book and doing whatever activity is on the page. For everyone, let it inspire your next Vegas vacation, staycation, or getaway!

Share your unique experiences and perspectives! Your stories are what make Las Vegas a dynamic city. Join my Las Vegas community on Instagram @shaundanecole to see what's happening in the City of Lights. Visit my travel site vegasrightnow.com for stories, pictures, and in-depth guides on things to do in Las Vegas today!

The Chandelier at The Cosmopolitan

FOOD AND DRINK

FEAST
ON SOUTHERN SOUL FOOD

I bet you didn't know Las Vegas is home to one of the most awarded soul food restaurants in the country. A place where the Southern fried chicken is so delicious it's become a legend! That place is Lo-Lo's Chicken & Waffles.

Let me share a personal story: When my best friend's mom, Grandma Pat, visited Las Vegas for the first time, she couldn't resist the temptation of Lo-Lo's famous fried chicken. She was so hooked that she ate there every day and even packed some chicken in her suitcase to take home. That's the kind of experience you can expect at Lo-Lo's!

As a proud native of the South and a soul food cookbook author and recipe creator, I can vouch for the authenticity of Lo-Lo's famous chicken and waffles, Southern banana pudding, collard greens, and red velvet cake. Each dish is a taste of home, a connection to my Southern roots.

325 Hughes Center Dr., 702-483-4311
loloschickenandwaffles.com

TIP

With only one Lo-Lo's in the entire Las Vegas Valley, it's more than just a restaurant. It's an experience! I suggest you order online to avoid the string of devoted customers, often extending outside the restaurant's door.

SAMPLE SOME SOUL FOOD

Discover more hidden gems of soul food on and near the Strip, each offering a unique culinary experience. This is not a complete list but rather a highlight of the city's many soulful eateries.

International Smoke

Inside MGM Grand, 3799 S Las Vegas Blvd.
internationalsmoke.com

Stuff My Turkey

4760 W Sahara Ave., Ste. 20, 702-530-1231
stuffmyturkeyusa.com

Streetbird by Chef Marcus Samuelsson

Inside Resorts World, 3000 S Las Vegas Blvd.
rwlasvegas.com/dining/streetbird

Yardbird

Inside the Venetian, 3355 S Las Vegas Blvd., 702-297-6541
runchickenrun.com/las-vegas

Mario's Westside Market

In the Historic Westside, 1425 W Lake Mead Blvd.
702-648-1482
marioswestsidemarket.com/menus

EMBRACE THE SPIRIT
OF INDULGENCE

Nevada's always been synonymous with endless plates thanks to the hundreds of casino buffets found in almost every town with a gambling station—from north to south in the Silver State, Reno to Las Vegas, and everywhere in between! Discover made-to-order choices, including seafood, decadent pastries, gelato, ice cream, and international cuisine. Why not celebrate the state with an indulgent feast in one of Vegas's world-famous buffets?

Get ready for a world of discovery, and leave your misconceptions of buffet dining at the door. Prepare to be astounded by the skill and talent of Las Vegas's chefs on display at the live-action cooking stations inside these lavish buffets!

Vegas buffet chefs bring the best dishes from around the globe, including Italian, Chinese, Japanese, Brazilian, and American cuisines. This plethora of delicious international dishes is a feast for the taste buds and the senses, including a wide range of choices made to order.

TIP

The buffets in Vegas are very popular, so making reservations is highly encouraged. If you can book in that sweet spot transitioning from lunch to dinner, you'll really get your money's worth with even more menu selections! Vegas buffets are also perfect for holiday dinners. You can feast on Thanksgiving, Christmas, or Easter with family and friends without washing dishes!

STEP UP TO A BUFFET

This is not a complete list but rather a highlight of the city's many favorite buffets.

The Buffet at Wynn

Inside Wynn Las Vegas, 3131 Las Vegas Blvd. S
702-770-3340
wynnlasvegas.com/dining/casual-dining/the-buffet

The Buffet at Bellagio

Inside Bellagio Hotel & Casino, 3600 Las Vegas Blvd. S
702-693-8112
bellagio.mgmresorts.com/en/restaurants/the-buffet

Wicked Spoon

Inside the Cosmopolitan of Las Vegas
3708 Las Vegas Blvd. S, Chelsea Tower, Level 2
877-893-2001
cosmopolitanlasvegas.mgmresorts.com/
en/restaurants/wicked-spoon

Bacchanal Buffet

Inside Caesar's Palace, 3570 Las Vegas Blvd. S
702-731-7928
caesars.com/caesars-palace/restaurants/bacchanal-buffet

Texas de Brazil

6533 Las Vegas Blvd. S, 702-605-7488
texasdebrazil.com/locations/las-vegas

A.Y.C.E. Buffet

Don't miss their all-you-can-eat lobster
nights and prime rib and snow crab buffets!
Inside Palms Casino Resort, 4321 W Flamingo Rd.
866-942-7777
palms.com/dining/ayce-buffet

EAT VEGAS'S
FAVORITE FOODS

What dessert is Nevada known for? Among the countless delicacies, one claims the status of Nevada's most beloved dessert: the distinctive and delightful Basque cheesecake. This treat captures the essence of the state's rich culinary heritage. It's a delicious link to the Basque immigrants. These pioneers brought their traditions to Nevada during the mid-19th-century mining rushes, leaving a lasting culinary legacy with this cheesecake.

If you've never tried Basque cheesecake, here's your chance! Order one of these Las Vegas favorite cakes from CasaMadrid by Churros. This bakery is the locals' preferred choice for an authentic Basque cheesecake made by a native Spaniard who's in constant contact with many bakers in Spain, including the owners of La Viña in San Sebastián, where the Basque cheesecake originated.

801-859-4400
churros101.com

TIP

What food is Las Vegas most known for? Surprise, surprise—it's a shrimp cocktail! This fancy seafood dish, which is said to have originated in Vegas in the 1950s, is a part of the city's rich culinary history. It's often presented in a martini glass with the shrimp hanging around the rim. (That's so Vegas!)

DINE IN AN ELEGANT TREE HOUSE
AT MASTRO'S OCEAN CLUB

Mastro's Ocean Club stands out even in Las Vegas with its architectural features and ambiance that redefine the dining experience. Imagine a tree house–like structure inside an upscale shopping mall. Mastro's is centrally positioned inside the Shops at Crystals, part of ARIA Campus (formerly CityCenter), the most expensive privately funded construction project in US history, costing nearly $9 billion. And yes, I said "privately" funded!

Positioned like a tree house made of handcrafted mahogany beams and extending between two floors, Mastro's welcomes you with twinkling lights and opulent decor, creating an atmosphere of refined dining luxury. Dinners here are unforgettable and a pampered experience, leaving you with memories of what was on your plate, plus an entire sensory journey!

3720 S Las Vegas Blvd., 702-798-7115
mastrosrestaurants.com/location/mastros-ocean-club-las-vegas

TIP

Everyone enters through the Tree House, and Mastro's enorces a strict upscale dress code. Their delectable and irresistible butter cake is a standout star on the menu. People come here just for that!

SECURE A SEAT AT THE TABLE
AT GOLDEN STEER STEAKHOUSE

Just off the renowned Las Vegas Strip, Golden Steer Steakhouse offers an unparalleled dining experience with exquisite surf and turf dishes. Since its establishment in 1958, this iconic restaurant has become a beloved fixture in the city's dining scene. It's celebrated for its colossal Australian lobster tails, enormous king crab legs, succulent prime rib, and awe-inspiring gigantic Tomahawk steaks.

Booking your table well in advance at the Golden Steer Steakhouse is not just a suggestion. It's a necessity. The restaurant's popularity often leads to it being fully booked months ahead, a clear indication of its high demand. Eager guests without reservations line up outside the restaurant before it opens, hoping to snag a coveted seat at the table!

The Steer's menu is so good that it's remained practically unchanged since the restaurant opened in 1958! A nostalgic highlight not to miss is that the immaculate seating booths are dedicated to various Vegas legends who were regular diners at the restaurant, including the Rat Pack, Elvis Presley, and Joe DiMaggio.

308 W Sahara Ave., 702-384-4470
goldensteer.com

STEP INTO THE WORLD OF SAM AND GINGER
FROM THE MOVIE *CASINO*

Nestled in the heart of neon-lit Las Vegas, the Peppermill Restaurant and Fireside Lounge is a testament to the city's timeless charm. This practically 24-hour diner, steeped in the rich history of Vegas's iconic eateries, is a journey back to the retro Vegas era, where scenes from the classic movie *Casino* were brought to life amid velvet booths and a flaming reflection pool. The Peppermill is a plush, nostalgic diner that still beautifully exists with old Vegas charm and a broad menu. Its romantic ambiance and retro decor transport you back to a time when Vegas nights were lit with neon lights, not smartphones.

The Peppermill is notably known for its appearance in the movie *Casino* as part of the world of Sam and Ginger. The film portrays the true story of mob influence on the Las Vegas hotel and casino scene during the 1970s. This legendary location has also been featured in other famous films, TV shows, and music videos, bringing the entertainment world to life.

2985 Las Vegas Blvd. S, 702-735-4177
peppermilllasvegas.com

EAT MICHELIN-STARRED
MEALS AT AFFORDABLE PRICES

Famous Foods Street Eats is nestled within the expansive, luxurious realm of Resorts World Las Vegas. This dining haven stands out for its decadent focus on internationally inspired street cuisine, including restaurants Ah Chun Shandong Dumpling and Geylang Claypot Rice, which have earned prestigious Michelin Star recognition. There's also James Beard Award–winning Chef Marcus Samuelsson's Streetbird restaurant, which offers a twist on Southern American comfort food classics. This multicultural food escape provides a tantalizing taste tour that spans continents without requiring a passport or a baller budget!

Famous Foods Street Eats is an affordable food court–style area with a vibrant mix of casual eateries and chic cafés. With more than 15 restaurants to choose from, this is your ticket to a passport-free journey across the world's most irresistible street food delicacies, all at prices that won't break the bank!

Famous Foods Street Eats
zoukgrouplc.com/famousfoods

RAISE A TOAST
AT VEGAS VALLEY WINERY

Vegas Valley Winery proudly holds the title of the first winery in the Las Vegas Valley! It offers diverse experiences, from community events to wine tastings, winery tours, and a unique selection of wine and hard cider. As a family-owned business, this pioneering winery is not just for wine enthusiasts but also for those who want to immerse themselves in local culture and connect with the community by introducing guests to wines bottled locally in the Vegas Valley. The winery is open seven days a week, inviting you to explore the art of wine making and enjoy the vibrant atmosphere filled with live music, wine-blending classes, and community partnerships.

7360 Eastgate Rd., Ste. 123, Henderson, 702-823-4065
vegasvalleywinery.com

TIP

Wineries are relatively new to Las Vegas! Before 2015, operating a winery in Nevada counties with a population of over 100,000 people was prohibited. Ordinarily, a crush pad is a place in a winery where grapes are turned into wine. Here in Las Vegas, it's a modern neighborhood wine bar for casual sips and a bottle shop, so you can take some home!

Crush Pad Wine Bar
7865 W Sahara Ave. Ste. #105, 702-848-2727, crushpadwinebar.com

---

TAKE A FOODIE
TASTING TOUR

Explore the larger-than-life casinos and their world-renowned restaurants along the Las Vegas Strip or in Downtown Las Vegas, and enjoy a decadent and wide-ranging tasting tour as you go! Vegas food tours are a fantastic and unique idea for effortlessly experiencing multiple five-star restaurants in one night. There's something for every taste and preference with various tour options, from self-guided tours to hosted tour experiences or limousine-chauffeured private parties.

The joy of dining in Las Vegas is not just in the eating but in discovering new attractions and restaurants and exploring new tastes. Tasting and food-sampling tours guide you through this culinary exploration, making every bite a new adventure. After all, one cannot survive on neon lights and high-stakes games alone. Sooner or later, you'll need to fuel up to keep up with the never-ending extravaganza that the City of Lights has to offer!

Lip Smacking Foodie Tours
lipsmackingfoodietours.com

Finger Licking Foodie Tours
fingerlickingfoodietours.com

Secret Food Tours
secretfoodtours.com/las-vegas

Soul Food On The Strip
thesoulfoodpot.com/
soul-food-on-the-strip

Food Tours of America
foodtoursofamerica.com/las-vegas

Taste Buzz Food Tours
tastebuzzvegas.com

HANG OUT WITH THE COOL CATS
AT THE CAT CAFÉ

A cat café is a unique form of entertainment that's sure to make you smile. And the Hearts Alive Village Cat Café (HAV Cat Café) is an attraction where you can watch and play with various cat breeds in a comfortable, cozy, communal café setting!

By scheduling an appointment and making a set entry donation, you can visit HAV Cat Café and enjoy an hour of snacks, beverages, a café seating area, Wi-Fi, and, of course, cuddles with adoptable cats! There are usually more than 50 feline friends in the café, classified as either friendly, not as social with humans, or not as friendly with other cats. Your donation helps cover the cost for a cat or kitten to receive a complete set of vaccines and a microchip, supporting their health and well-being.

1750 S Rainbow Blvd., #4, 702-870-0065
heartsalivevillage.org/cat-cafe

TIP

And here's the best part: If you decide to adopt one of the café cats, your entrance donation will be deducted from the adoption fee!
Another Vegas café that's also the cat's meow?
Rescued Treasures Cat Café
4155 N Rancho Dr., #150, 702-629-6351, palnv.org

HOP THROUGH
VEGAS'S BREWERIES

Las Vegas has brewed up a reputation for more than just its dazzling slots and neon lights. This desert oasis has become a haven for craft beer enthusiasts, blooming with numerous brewery tasting rooms that cater to every palate. Breweries like Big Dog's Brewing Company and Las Vegas Brewing Company have poured their hearts into creating drinks and experiences, setting the stage for a citywide craft beer renaissance. At the same time, Beer Zombies and Able Baker Brewing Company push boundaries with unique blends and seasonal beers.

Big Dog's Brewing Company
4543 N Rancho Dr.
702-645-1404
bigdogsbrews.com

Beer Zombies Brewing Co.
831 W Bonanza Rd.
702-362-7335
thebeerzombies.com

Las Vegas Brewing Company
3101 N Tenaya Way
702-333-4858
lvbrewco.com

Able Baker Brewing Company
1510 S Main St., Ste. #120
702-479-6355
ablebakerbrewing.com

TIP

Unlock the behind-the-scenes of Las Vegas breweries on a brewery tour, a unique experience offering a peek behind the curtain of craft beer brewing in the heart of Vegas. Be sure to check out the many craft brewers on Brewery Row in Downtown Las Vega!

Grab a map: lasvegasnevada.gov/news/blog/detail/brewery-row

BREWERIES

Can't make it to Germany for Oktoberfest?

No worries! You can experience it every day of the week in Las Vegas at Hofbräuhaus. It's the only place where beer lovers can taste Germany's oldest beer—the same one served at the Oktoberfest in Munich, Germany! This lively Oktoberfest celebration offers classic Bavarian beer brewed according to the Purity Law of 1516, complemented by a featured selection of mouthwatering authentic Bavarian dishes.

Hofbräuhaus Las Vegas
4510 Paradise Rd., 702-853-2337
hofbrauhauslasvegas.com

Looking for $2 beers in Las Vegas?

You're in luck! $2 beers have become an iconic tradition in the city, symbolizing its dedication to offering unparalleled value to visitors. Stage Door Casino is known as Vegas's favorite no-frills dive bar. With the tagline "Where the drinks are cheap and the machines are loose," it's open 24/7 and is known for its odd-numbered $1 and $3 beers!

Stage Door Casino
4000 Linq Ln., 702-733-0124
stagedoorcasino.com

BRING FIDO WITH YOU
TO LAZY DOG RESTAURANT & BAR

Canine critics rate Lazy Dog Restaurant in Las Vegas two paws up because you can bring your furry friend along! This pet-friendly restaurant has a laid-back, indoor/outdoor lodge-style setting. It serves a variety of comfort foods such as burgers, wings, hummus, brussels sprouts, deviled eggs, and banana pudding. And the best part? They have a large patio with a canopy cover and zipper enclosure where your dog can relax and dine with you!

Check out Lazy Dog's website for their pooch patio rules before you go. These simple guidelines include not placing dogs on the table (because the health department says so) and keeping dogs on a leash to ensure they remain welcome at this inclusive restaurant.

1725 Festival Plaza Dr., 702-727-4784,
and 6509 Las Vegas Blvd., 702-941-1920
lazydogrestaurants.com

TIP

Lazy Dog offers a dine-in dog menu, plus another convenient option for busy pet parents. You can also take home chef-prepared retro-style TV dinners to pop in the oven when needed.

For homemade doggie bags to go, grab a Dog Meal at Fido's Kitchen!

7875 W Sahara Ave., Ste. 103, 702-869-0520, fidoskitchenusa.com

---

COOL OFF FROM THE DESERT HEAT
AT MINUS5° ICE BAR

Escape the scorching triple-digit Vegas heat and step into minus5° Ice Bar, where the temperature is a refreshing minus 5! This icy wonderland, adorned with over 90 tons of ice, features stunning ice sculptures that shimmer under the lights. Themed rooms transport you into a world far removed from the desert heat outside. Here, you can enjoy the unique experience of sipping cocktails from liquor glasses made entirely of ice. To keep warm, minus5° lends parkas and gloves. Or opt for the "V-ICE-P" opulent occasion with faux fur coats.

Even though minus5° boasts specialty cocktails, clubby music, and LED lights, the coolest experience in Las Vegas is also for kids, including a souvenir gift and an icy mocktail drink!

Note that minus5° has three convenient locations on the Las Vegas Strip: minus5° inside Mandalay Bay, the Venetian, and the LINQ Promenade.

702-586-8925
minus5experience.com

UNVEIL A CULINARY CURTAIN CALL
WITH DINNER AND A SHOW

Las Vegas, a city that's mastered the art of blending fine dining with entertainment, offers exclusive dinner shows that are a privilege to experience. Dinner shows here captivate audiences with a fusion never seen in other destinations. You can enjoy dining experiences surrounded by legends. From Motown performers at Alexis Park to medieval knights at Excalibur Hotel to an off-the-wall house party at the Cosmopolitan's *Superfrico*, each dining experience is a rare and spectacular event that will leave you in awe of the brilliance of the shows.

By combining Las Vegas entertainment with a culinary adventure, you're making a savvy move to maximize your trip. The top shows in the city are in high demand and can sell out quickly, so booking your dinner shows in advance is a proactive step that can save you from disappointment.

VEGAS DINNER SHOW FAVORITES

All Motown
Alexis Park Resort Hotel, 375 E Harmon Ave.
modernvegas.com/show/all-motown

Tournament of Kings
Excalibur Hotel & Casino, 3850 S Las Vegas Blvd.
excalibur.mgmresorts.com/en/entertainment/
tournament-of-kings

Superfrico
The Cosmopolitan of Las Vegas
3708 Las Vegas Blvd. S, Chelsea Tower, Level 2
spiegelworld.com/restaurants/superfrico

The Mayfair Supper Club
Bellagio Hotel & Casino, 3600 Las Vegas Blvd. S
bellagio.mgmresorts.com/en/restaurants/
the-mayfair-supperclub

House of Blues
Mandalay Bay Resort and Casino
3950 S Las Vegas Blvd.
houseofblues.com/lasvegas

Marriage Can Be Murder
The Orleans Hotel & Casino, 4500 W Tropicana Ave.
marriagecanbemurder.com

Vegas! The Show
Miracle Mile Shops inside Planet Hollywood Las Vegas
Resort & Casino, 3663 Las Vegas Blvd. S, Ste. #454
vegastheshow.com

Lake of Dreams
Wynn Las Vegas, 3131s Las Vegas Blvd. S
wynnlasvegas.com/entertainment/lake-of-dreams

DINE ABOVE
THE LAS VEGAS STRIP

Step into the city's vibrant atmosphere through Las Vegas's most spectacular rooftop restaurants and bars. It's an unforgettable blend of natural beauty and urban elegance. Enjoy the mesmerizing sunset over the Vegas Strip, indulge in luxury dining, and savor delicious meals while basking in panoramic city lights and desert landscape views.

Whether it's a romantic sunset dinner on the rooftop at The W Las Vegas's award-winning restaurant Rivea or an electrifying nightlife experience on the patio of Ghostbar and its skyline views of Red Rock Canyon and Downtown Las Vegas, it's an experience as sweet as dessert, delivering a stunning backdrop and promising an evening filled with excitement and thrill.

SOME OF VEGAS'S HIGH-ALTITUDE DINING SPOTS

Ghostbar
4321 W Flamingo Rd., 866-942-7777
palms.com/dining/ghostbar

Rivea
3940 S Las Vegas Blvd., 877-632-5400
wlasvegas.mgmresorts.com/en/restaurants/rivea.html

Top of the World
2000 Las Vegas Blvd. S, 702-380-7711
thestrat.com/restaurants/top-of-the-world

Ole Red Las Vegas
3627 S Las Vegas Blvd., 725-303-1818
olered.com/lasvegas

Eiffel Tower Restaurant
3655 Las Vegas Blvd. S, 702-948-6937
eiffeltowerrestaurant.com

Beer Park
3655 Las Vegas Blvd. S, 702-444-4500
beerpark.com

BrewDog
3767 Las Vegas Blvd. S, 702-331-7516
brewdog.com/usa/las-vegas

Commonwealth
525 E Fremont St., 702-445-6400
commonwealthlv.com

Liftoff Bar & Ride
3215 S Rancho Dr.
area15.com/eat-drink/liftoff-bar-and-ride

TOAST TO THE GOOD LIFE
AT A BOOZY BRUNCH

In Las Vegas, brunch transforms into an unforgettable extravaganza! This city, famed for its boundless energy and penchant for indulgence, elevates the brunch experience to new heights. A weekend in Vegas promises more than a meal. It delivers an event by merging gourmet brunch menus with the allure of bottomless mimosas, mimosa flights, Bloody Marys, rosé, and Aperol spritzes! The vibrant backdrop of Vegas, with its sunlit patios and poolside venues, provides the perfect scene for leisurely sipping brunch cocktails.

TIP

Enjoying brunch by the lake, pool, or at a drag show adds a memorable touch to the Vegas boozy brunch experience. Some notable places to enjoy this are the Cosmopolitan's Overlook Grill with poolside views, Americana Restaurant with lakeside views, and Alexxa's at Paris with Fountains of Bellagio show views!

Lakeside View

Americana Restaurant
2620 Regatta Dr., Ste. #118, 702-331-5565
americanalasvegas.com

Fountains of Bellagio Views

Alexxa's at Paris
3655 S Las Vegas Blvd., 702-331-5100
alexxaslasvegas.com

Poolside Views

Overlook Grill at the Cosmopolitan
Boulevard Tower, 3708 Las Vegas Blvd. S, 702-698-7970
cosmopolitanlasvegas.mgmresorts.com/
en/restaurants/overlook-grill

Drag Brunch Shows

Señor Frog's at Treasure Island
3300 Las Vegas Blvd. S, 702-912-9525
treasureisland.com/restaurants/senor-frogs

Hamburger Mary's Las Vegas
1700 E Flamingo Rd., 702-592-0208
hamburgermarys.com/lasvegas

Boozy Brunch Locals' Favorites

Makers & Finders
1120 S Main St., Ste. 110, and 2120 Festival
Plaza Dr., Unit 140, 702-586-8255
makerslv.com

Café Lola
3500 S Las Vegas Blvd. + multiple locations, 702-760-5652
ilovecafelola.com

Hash House A Go Go
3535 Las Vegas Blvd. S + multiple locations, 702-254-4646
hashhouseagogo.com

SCOOP UP
THE LAS VEGAS ICE CREAM SCENE

Las Vegas, a city celebrated for its culinary eccentricities, boasts an ice cream scene that is as varied and dazzling as its nightlife. This desert oasis is home to many ice cream shops, each offering its unique take on ice cream, frozen custard, and artisanal Italian gelato.

From the nostalgia-invoking flavors of the Fruit Boat or Western sundae at Luv-It Frozen Custard to the innovative exotic concoctions of ube and lychee at Lappert's Ice Cream. Or Sloan's Ice Cream's festive-themed sundaes, such as the Sandcastle Sundae which involves filling a beach sand pail complete with a shovel and their epic Tracy's Kitchen Sink—the ice cream works, all served in an actual sink! This diversity turns each visit into a voyage of discovery, ensuring every palate finds its match in a flavor to adore.

Lappert's Ice Cream
Inside California Hotel & Casino
12 E Ogden Ave., #2F
702-385-1222
lapperts.com

Sloan's Ice Cream
Inside the Venetian
3377 S Las Vegas Blvd., Ste. 2255
702-776-6200
sloansicecream.com

Luv-It Frozen Custard
505 E Oakey Blvd., 702-384-6452
luvitfrozencustard.com

INDULGE IN A FAIRY-TALE BRUNCH
AT THE GARDEN TABLE

Prepare to be enchanted by the fairy-tale brunch at the Garden Table in Bellagio Hotel & Casino. Situated in the hotel's breathtaking conservatory and botanical gardens, the Garden Table offers an exclusive single-table dining experience amid a 14,000-square-foot flowering seasonal showcase. Whether it's brunch or dinner, reservations are a must to ensure you don't miss out on this unique experience. If the Garden Table is fully booked, Sadelle's Café is a delightful alternative that also offers an upscale brunch overlooking the botanical gardens, so be sure to secure your spot there!

The Garden Table
3600 Las Vegas Blvd. S, 702-693-7075
bellagio.mgmresorts.com/en/restaurants/the-garden-table.html

TIP

After brunch or dinner, visit Vanderpump Cocktail Garden in Caesars Palace for a glamorous cocktail experience in an exquisite floral setting created by renowned restaurateur Lisa Vanderpump.

3570 Las Vegas Blvd. S, 702-731-7867
caesars.com/caesars-palace/things-to-do/nightlife/vanderpump

DISCOVER
LAS VEGAS'S CANDY LAND

Las Vegas offers attractions that go beyond the ordinary, and the Ethel M Chocolates Factory is a prime example.

Who is Ethel M? Ethel Mars was the mother of the Mars Incorporated chocolate empire. In 1978, Ethel's son, Forrest Mars Sr., retired from the family business and moved to Las Vegas to pursue his passion for cacti and to grow a cactus garden. Mars got bored of retirement and opened the premium Ethel M Chocolates Factory, paying homage to his mother. As the luxury tier of the Mars family brand, the chocolates here are made in small batches, free of artificial preservatives, packaged and boxed right on-site!

The chocolate artisans at Mars excel in creating small-batch chocolates, always prioritizing quality. Their family-friendly experiences are enriched with educational factory-viewing aisles, where you can witness the chocolate-making process firsthand. It's a rare glimpse into the dedication and craftsmanship behind the premium Ethel M Chocolates.

2 Cactus Garden Dr., Henderson
ethelm.com

TIP

Forrest Mars Sr. pursued his passion for cacti by establishing the largest cactus garden in Nevada! The impressive Botanical Cactus Garden spans over three acres on the Ethel M Chocolates flagship store campus and is open for visitors to explore. It's a place you won't want to miss, especially on Valentine's Day and Christmas, as the massive garden lights up for the holidays!

If you're looking for chocolate on the Las Vegas Strip, Ethel M's satellite store can satisfy your cravings. You'll also find other Las Vegas–style beloved candy store offerings.

M&M's Las Vegas
3785 S Las Vegas Blvd., 702-740-2504
mms.com/en-us/explore/mms-stores/las-vegas

Hershey's Chocolate World Las Vegas
3790 S Las Vegas Blvd., 702-437-7439
hersheyschocolateworldlasvegas.com

I Love Sugar
3545 S Las Vegas Blvd., Ste. L-28, 702-699-5443
ilovesugar.com

Sugar Factory
3717 S Las Vegas Blvd., 725-777-1216
sugarfactory.com

Sphere

MUSIC
AND ENTERTAINMENT

WITNESS THE
SPHERE EXPERIENCE
IN PERSON

Everyone on the planet seems to be talking about Sphere! A one-of-a-kind, never-before-done 366-foot-tall and 516-foot-wide spherical marvel strategically positioned just east of the Las Vegas Strip.

Fun fact: My neighbor helped build it!

There's the Vegas you're used to, and then there's this! Sphere. A concert venue, theater, event space, and enormous, magnificent attraction. With its impressive size and the world's largest LED screen, this colossal black orb has redefined the boundaries of architecture, design, and technology. The exterior curve of Sphere spans over 580,000 square feet, equivalent to 10 American football fields!

TIP

It's absolutely free to witness the stunning displays at the Sphere, featuring its constantly changing 360-degree screen display. Its a particularly spectacular site during the holidays and special events. It does cost to go inside for a concert or Sphere's inspiring movie and tour, part of the Sphere Experience. Buy concert tickets, schedule a tour, or visit for the best views!

255 Sands Ave., 725-258-6724, thesphere.com

WALK THE ENTIRE
LAS VEGAS STRIP

Despite all the excitement surrounding Las Vegas and the city's unprecedented number of casinos, neon signs, and extraordinary world-famous reputation, family, friends, and first-time visitors still ask me, "What is the Las Vegas Strip?" In short, the Strip is *the* place to be! Even though the Strip is only a fraction of this dynamic city, it's still a significant chunk to see.

The Las Vegas Strip, a grand and well-known street called Las Vegas Boulevard, spans 4.2 miles. It starts on the north end at the STRAT Hotel near Sahara Avenue and ends at the iconic Welcome to Fabulous Las Vegas Sign just past the Mandalay Bay Hotel on the south end. Despite its relatively short distance, the Strip is a hotbed of activity, attracting a staggering 40-plus-million visitors annually (and counting)! With its towering resorts, sprawling casinos, and endless entertainment options, each hotel on the Strip has its own personality and offers a unique experience.

You may be interested in walking the entire Las Vegas Strip and want to know how long it would take. But there's no easy way to say. Your walking pace, the stops you make along the way, the Monorail or express trams you might use, or weather conditions can all influence your journey. But if you walk continuously at a moderate pace without stopping, crossing the entire Las Vegas Strip would take approximately four to five hours! The unpredictability adds to the thrill and adventure of exploring this iconic boulevard.

vegasrightnow.com/what-is-the-las-vegas-strip

STOP TO SMELL THE FLOWERS
AND WATCH THE DANCING WATERS

The Fountains of Bellagio is a one-of-a-kind, 1,000-foot water show that is the main attraction in front of the iconic Bellagio Hotel & Casino. This unique show features water streams that dance in a harmonious fusion of advanced technology and meticulous design, creating a stunning aquatic masterpiece. High-powered jets synchronize perfectly with popular musical scores, sending water shooting into the sky and giving the performance an awe-inspiring vertical dimension.

3600 Las Vegas Blvd. S
bellagio.mgmresorts.com

TIP

Another elaborate must-see is the grand Bellagio Conservatory & Botanical Gardens. It's themed according to the season and covers 14,000 square feet! The gardens offer stunning sights, sounds, scents, and colors in an airy and spacious indoor greenhouse. The ever-changing display has included waterfalls, bridges over water, swimming koi fish, hot-air balloons, and larger-than-life flowers.

The Fountains of Bellagio and botanical gardens are open all day and night, welcoming you to enjoy these complimentary Las Vegas shows at your convenience.

ENJOY FREE DRINKS
WHILE GAMBLING

Las Vegas, situated in the desert, features a plethora of casinos instead of a plentiful water supply. If you're at least 21, you can enjoy the thrill of gambling here!

You'll see casinos at the airport, gas stations, grocery stores, neighborhood pubs, residential resorts, and almost every hotel property along the Strip. Vegas has more than 100 casinos, from its suburbs to Downtown Las Vegas to Fremont Street and the Strip.

You can expect to receive free drinks when gambling, a long-standing tradition that may have originated in Las Vegas. Cocktail servers typically visit each table or slot every 20–30 minutes. As long as you remain at your table or slot machine and keep playing, the servers will continue to bring you drinks free of charge! This can include nonalcoholic beverages like soda and water and alcohol options like cocktails and beer. It's customary to tip the cocktail servers generously.

TIP
It may come as a surprise that there are hotels without casinos on the Vegas Strip, including Vdara, Four Seasons, and the Signature at MGM Grand.

EXPLORE PAST AND PRESENT-DAY LAS VEGAS
ON FREMONT STREET

The Fremont Street Experience is distinctly different from the famous Las Vegas Strip due to its seamless blend of historical significance and modern-day marvels. Right in the heart of Downtown Las Vegas, it offers a unique charm created by the coexistence of the past and the present.

Attractions on Fremont Street include the world's largest LED canopy, the Viva Vision Light Show (which is 1,375 feet long) and the 77-foot-tall adrenaline-pumping SlotZilla Zipline. New hotel addition Circa boasts the world's largest sportsbook with an impressive three stories to place your bets! Meanwhile, Stadium Swim, Fremont Street's awe-inspiring rooftop pool in an amphitheater setting, further enhances the area's appeal.

This famous street offers diverse entertainment, from free nightly concerts to legendary hotels, renowned casinos, vintage Vegas restaurants, and shopping. Take a leisurely stroll and enjoy talented street performers at the Freemont Street Experience—note that tipping is customary but entirely voluntary—and enjoy the neon-lit history of iconic Vegas hotels like the Golden Gate and Golden Nugget. Explore all this for free!

Fremont St.
vegasexperience.com

TIP

Adults 21 and over can walk Fremont Street with alcohol in a plastic cup, but open bottles are not permitted. Many visitors enjoy the talented street performers at the Fremont Street Experience. Still, they might not know that street performers cannot ask for a fee. So, tipping is customary but entirely voluntary.

UNLOCK ELITE STATUS
WITH A CASINO REWARDS PROGRAM

Las Vegas thrives on the allure of status, and its casino loyalty programs are the golden ticket. Guests can unlock a diverse world of perks by engaging with MGM Rewards, Caesars Rewards, or other resorts' programs. These perks can include free parking and waived resort fees to comped rooms and free cruises, demonstrating that heavy investment in gambling, dining, and hotel stays can pay off generously! Elevating your status to Gold or Platinum tiers amplifies benefits, like exclusive events and discounts. Participation in these rewards programs enhances the overall Vegas experience beyond mere gambling, offering a variety of rewards to keep you excited.

TIP
There are many more casino loyalty programs to explore from Vegas resorts on and off the Strip, including Station Casinos, Venetian and Palazzo, Resorts World, Wynn and Encore, SAHARA, Palms, and Fontainebleau. Each unfurls a unique tapestry of rewards, catering to a diverse visitor base that includes high rollers, casual gamblers, and those who simply enjoy the Vegas experience.

FEEL THE ENERGY UP CLOSE
AT A VEGAS RESIDENCY

A Vegas residency is your golden ticket to performances by world-class superstars on your vacation! This concept involves entertainment legends headlining multiple shows at a given venue over some time. From Mr. Las Vegas Wayne Newton to the timeless melodies of Barry Manilow, Adele's soulful voice, and the electrifying talents of Bruno Mars, the residency scene is a melting pot of iconic artists who draw crowds to a single concert venue throughout the year. Residency theaters and coliseums are spacious yet intimate, allowing you to feel the show's energy up close. You may even feel part of the performance as your favorite artists engage directly with their crowds.

TIP

There are usually no bad seats in the Vegas residency house. The venues are designed to ensure that every seat provides a great view and an immersive experience. The goal is just to be there, and you can rest assured that you'll have a great view from wherever you're seated!

PARTY WITH THE WORLD'S
TOP DJS

Las Vegas is famous for its star-studded residencies, which include performing artists, musicians, and some of the world's top DJs. These touring DJs have a vast and dedicated following that plays a crucial role in the city's vibrant nightlife and day pool club scenes. In Vegas, "The party don't start 'til the DJ steps in!" Whether for nightclub appearances or show residencies.

Top DJs who perform in Vegas include Pauly D, Steve Aoki, Diplo, and Marshmello; Anderson .Paak performs under his DJ alter ego, DJ Pee .Wee. Headliners like D-Nice and DJ Cassidy also take center stage for live concerts. The Vegas party scene has a unique energy and appeal, thanks to the city's deep affection for professional disc jockeys.

TIP

Las Vegas is home to several celebrities, including DJ Pauly D, Steve Aoki, Flavor Flav, hometown-hero band Imagine Dragons, and heavyweights Mike Tyson and Floyd Mayweather Jr. You might also run into Carrot Top, Criss Angel, Carlos Santana, or Celine Dion offstage in the city. It's common to spot these superstars at Vegas nightclubs and DJ-hosted events. Keep an eye on celebrity DJ parties and tour schedules and check their websites and social media for updates on ticket availability.

HONOR THE LEGENDS
AT A TRIBUTE SHOW

Las Vegas has earned its title as the Entertainment Capital of the World. On this sacred ground, legends like the Rat Pack, Tony Bennett, Michael Jackson, and Prince once performed and held court. Fans worldwide come to experience the magic of live entertainment that commemorates these music icons. These unforgettable performances offer a rare chance to relive once-in-a-lifetime concerts, now re-created through tribute shows featuring live bands and spectacular impersonators with a commitment to the original performances.

Tribute shows cater to every music lover, from fans of the electrifying performances of the Beatles and Tina Turner to enthusiasts of the smooth tunes of the Australian Bee Gees. Elvis tribute acts stand out, drawing tourists eager for a glimpse of the King's legendary stage presence. Each act, celebrated for its authenticity and dynamic performance, makes up the vibrant Viva Las Vegas entertainment scene, ensuring that the spirit of these legendary musicians continues to resonate on the Strip.

TIP

For those seeking last-minute Vegas entertainment and shows, consider using discount ticket outlets like Tix4Vegas. They offer convenient ticket sales at unbeatable prices. You can purchase online or visit one of their several locations on the Las Vegas Strip. Find more information at tix4vegas.com.

EXPERIENCE THE VEGAS VIBE
AT A MUSIC FESTIVAL

Las Vegas, a city famous for its electrifying nightlife, hosts a variety of music festivals catering to diverse tastes. Events like Sick New World bring back hard rock sounds with nu metal, while Lovers & Friends celebrates the golden era of R & B and hip-hop. On the other hand, Punk Rock Bowling injects a dose of punk, ska, and rock, while EDC thrills with pulsating club beats. These festivals enrich Las Vegas's entertainment lineup and attract music lovers worldwide, offering unique experiences that resonate with a wide range of musical tastes. Las Vegas festivals usually take place in the spring, skipping the hotter summer months and resuming in the fall, so plan your trip accordingly!

For more information, visit:
musicfestivalwizard.com/festival-guide/las-vegas

TIP

When attending a festival in Las Vegas, it's crucial to stay hydrated and pack wisely. Essentials like comfortable footwear, sunscreen, sunglasses, and a hat for daytime events are your best friends on the festival scene! These steps are your ticket to a smooth festival experience in the heart of the Las Vegas sunshine and heat.

SASHAY
AT RUPAUL'S LIVE SHOW

Straight outta your TV screens and live onstage at the Flamingo Hotel in fabulous Las Vegas, *RuPaul's Drag Race LIVE!* is a vibrant showcase of Pride culture. Experience the thrill of this live performance as you "Sashay Shantay" with a rotating cast of the world's most famous show queens! In their elaborate costumes, the queens dance to their favorite energetic top hits and original show songs, creating a competition that's even better than you've seen on TV!

This Las Vegas show is a true embodiment of RuPaul's vision, celebrating Pride performances, humor, and heart in a live performance setting. It's a celebration that not only entertains but also makes a profound statement on the importance and influence of LGBTQ+ culture in the mainstream community and beyond. It's an inclusive show and a welcoming space for all to enjoy!

3555 Las Vegas Blvd. S
caesars.com/flamingo-las-vegas/shows/rupauls-drag-race-live

TIP

After the show, don't miss RuPaul's "Werk Room" inside Flamingo Las Vegas. This is the show's official merch store, where you enter a dressing room with a treasure chest full of glittering rainbow finds and the best Pride-chic merch. It's the perfect way to keep the show's spirit alive even after the curtains close!

LOUNGE WITH BRUNO MARS
IN 24K LUXURY

Step into the world of Bruno Mars's Pinky Ring lounge, an ultra-exclusive VIP venue nestled within the Bellagio Hotel & Casino. This intimate music venue and cocktail lounge is a quintessential Las Vegas experience. Yet, it stands in a league of its own, a symbol of exclusivity, as every 24K detail, from the mid-century modern furnishings to the hand-picked cocktail menu, has been selected by the modern-day Mr. Las Vegas himself, Bruno Mars.

Despite being within the Bellagio, the Pinky Ring has no on-site kitchen for appetizers or meals. This unique approach sets it apart, allowing the lounge to focus on its exceptional menu of original drinks, expertly crafted with beverages named after each of the Hooligans' band members.

3600 Las Vegas Blvd. S, 702-693-8393
vegasrightnow.com/bruno-mars-pinky-ring

TIP

Connect with the present moment at the Pinky Ring, where a "No phones allowed" policy is in place. This rule is not a restriction but a liberating invitation to live in the moment. No pictures or videos are permitted, creating an enclave where every moment is cherished and remembered, not just recorded.

LAUGH OUT LOUD
AT JIMMY KIMMEL'S COMEDY CLUB

The Las Vegas Jimmy Kimmel's Comedy Club and its roster make Las Vegas's entertainment scene richer. As someone who grew up in Las Vegas, Kimmel has dedicated himself to live entertainment and provides a platform for both established and up-and-coming comedians. The club's cozy and inviting atmosphere captures the essence of Las Vegas nightlife. At the same time, its full menu of casual cuisine, shareable bites, and happy hour specials ensures a complete Vegas dining and entertainment experience.

The comedy club is located in the modern shopping, dining, and entertainment district at LINQ Promenade on the Strip. The intimate showroom can accommodate up to 300 guests with various seating choices. As is common in comedy clubs, no photography, video, or audio recording is allowed in the venue at any time to show respect for the comedians and their performances.

TIP

Don't miss out on the funny and the fun! Check the venue's website for the weekly comedian lineup and monthly headliners. To secure the best seats, book early before they sell out.

3545 Las Vegas Blvd. S, 855-234-7469
jimmykimmelscomedyclub.com

CATCH A BROADWAY SHOW
AT THE SMITH CENTER

The Smith Center for the Performing Arts in Downtown Las Vegas is just a few miles past the Strip's bright neon lights, incredible concerts, residencies, music festivals, and gravity-defying shows. Adding a different layer of entertainment offerings, the Smith Center is the ideal place to enjoy Broadway shows, top musicals, dance performances, concerts, and theater productions. Nestled in Vegas's 61-acre Symphony Park, this five-acre performing arts center comprises three theaters in two buildings, offering ample space for a variety of shows.

Enjoy *The Cher Show*, *Back to the Future: The Musical*, *Shrek the Musical*, *The Wiz*, and *Hamilton*, as well as local productions featuring the Las Vegas Philharmonic or the Nevada Ballet Theatre. The center hosts concerts with world-renowned artists offering classical, pop, rock, jazz, multicultural performances, dance, and talks by influential speakers.

While Las Vegas has long been hailed as the Entertainment Capital of the World, the inauguration of the Smith Center in 2012 truly solidified its status. This leading performing arts center, on par with those found in other great cities worldwide, has elevated the city's cultural scene to new heights.

361 Symphony Park Ave., 702-749-2000
thesmithcenter.com

TIP

The Smith Center is a technical work of art. Its state-of-the-art facilities enable high-tech advancements and amenities to accommodate the latest attractions and showcase the finest acoustics for soloists. This venue takes the Las Vegas show experience to a whole new level. It's a must-visit for anyone looking for a masterful performance.

True to a Las Vegas–style dinner and show, you can enjoy fine wine, champagne, spirits, snacks, and casual dining at several bars and lounges in the various theater halls.

RING IN THE NEW YEAR
IN LAS VEGAS

New Year's Eve in Las Vegas is an exhilarating experience as the city becomes a dazzling display of lights, fireworks, fantastic concerts, and lively celebrations. This is the night this town waits all year for, to do what Las Vegas does best—and that's throw the biggest party!

Exclusive parties are hosted by celebrity DJs and music artists, offering VIP packages that usually include a midnight champagne toast, gourmet bites, and unobstructed views of the fireworks display. This is the night to be in Vegas, where you can let loose and enjoy the festivities. After all, there are 364 other days to go to bed early!

TIP

Most New Year's Eve concerts and shows in Vegas typically end around 11 p.m., allowing you plenty of time to join the official countdown celebration on the Las Vegas Strip.

No one knows what the Sphere will do next. So, don't miss its live show on New Year's Eve. It might surprise us all with its own countdown and impressive fireworks display!

Attend cultural celebrations such as the Chinese New Year, which features annual festivals and parades throughout the city. A seasonal display for the Lunar New Year can also be found on the Strip at the Bellagio Conservatory & Botanical Gardens.

STEP INTO THE FUTURE
OF DIGITAL MEMORABILIA

Three-hundred-sixty-degree spin cams are the newest attraction on the Vegas Strip! These outdoor photo booth experiences capture you, your family, or your friends having a great time against the iconic Las Vegas Strip's skyline, spinning around you in a 360-degree view. At the same time, you remain the point of focus throughout. Typically, the camera moves, but you and your group stay on a stationary platform. However, dancing and having a good time are musts!

Like a TikTok or an Instagram Reel, the footage takes less than 30 seconds to capture. Thanks to state-of-the-art technology, it's sent to your smartphone in less than a minute. This quick turnaround ensures you can share your immersive content with friends and family in no time. With digital memorabilia, moments as lively and energetic as the Las Vegas Strip are easily preserved.

TIP

Each 360-degree spin cam vendor charges a different price for this video experience. However, I've learned that you can negotiate for the best price.

SWIM UP TO VEGAS NIGHTLIFE
IN BROAD DAYLIGHT

Las Vegas day clubs are not just any pool party. They're an exclusive VIP experience only found in Vegas. It's like having the city's vibrant nightlife brought to you in broad daylight, making you feel like a true insider!

Among the many Las Vegas day clubs, Sammy's Island stands out. Nestled within the vibrant Palms Casino Resort, it's a tropical oasis shaped by the legendary rocker Sammy Hagar of Van Halen fame. His passion for the tropical lifestyle is evident in every corner of this unique day club.

At Sammy's Island, you'll find a tropical beach resort experience like no other. Multiple island-style pools, a DJ on stage playing all the hits, private cabanas and bungalows with sofa-sectional lounging and flat-screen TVs, private glass balcony pools, Vegas-style food, tiki bars, a dining area, and the most attentive resort service and staff. And the best part? Free parking!

Vegas day clubs are famous for their unique blend of relaxation and thrills. They offer an exciting and unique experience with the refreshing coolness of water. Get ready to be intrigued!

4321 W Flamingo Rd.
palms.com/experiences/palms-pool

SOME OF VEGAS'S MANY POPULAR DAY CLUBS

AYU Dayclub at Resorts World
Flamingo Go Pool
Encore Beach Club
Bel-Aire Backyard at Durango
Palm Tree Beach Club at MGM Grand
Liquid Pool Lounge at ARIA
TAO Beach Dayclub at the Venetian
DAYLIGHT Beach Club at Mandalay Bay
Marquee Dayclub at the Cosmopolitan
Drai's Beachclub at the Cromwell
LIV Beach at Fontainebleau
Venus Pool + Lounge at Caesars Palace

TIP

Las Vegas pool season is a thrilling experience that starts earlier and lasts longer than other tourist destinations. It begins annually in March and goes on until October. Day clubs with a lively atmosphere, DJ sets, and festivities require guests to be 21 and over. Many of these Vegas pools have an entry fee similar to a nightclub, and the VIP tables at these daytime events are the luxury-priced coveted cabanas!

INVITE FRIENDS
TO A DISCO PARTY IN THE BATHROOM

It's a potty. And a party! Tucked away at the heart of Resorts World Las Vegas lies a hidden gem that ignites curiosity and excitement—the Disco Party Bathroom! It's like stumbling upon a secret Vegas speakeasy or a Las Vegas secret hotel. The Disco Party Bathroom is a thrilling surprise, hiding in plain sight yet reserved for only a select few to find.

An influencer favorite, this Disco Bathroom is a novelty and an incredibly functional attraction showcasing Resorts World's innovative amenities. It's a space where you can have fun and freshen up at the same time. Imagine an entryway with enough room to form a *Soul Train* line under strobe lights, disco balls, and holographic walls sparkling from ceiling to floor. Party tracks play in the background, further energizing the space. This lavish lavatory is a must-visit for anyone who wants to experience the sheer vibrancy and energy of Las Vegas at every turn and angle during their stay!

3000 S Las Vegas Blvd.
vegasrightnow.com/disco-party-bathroom

TIP

Where is it? The Disco Party Bathroom is in Resorts World's Famous Foods Street Eats food court, across from the main casino floor. Now that you know, it'll be hard to miss this restroom's neon glow!

FIND A HIDDEN
SPEAKEASY BAR

These are some of the best, worst-kept secrets in Las Vegas! Hidden speakeasy bars—the tantalizing secrets beyond the neon lights. Surprisingly, these covert venues are not hiding underground. They're quietly tucked away from the eyes of the casual observer. But for those with curiosity and a discerning eye, they're a thrilling discovery in plain sight!

Brimming with Prohibition-era charm while managing to infuse a dash of modern mixology, today's speakeasies sometimes require a password. In contrast, others only require a curious eye to look beyond the inconspicuous door. From barbershops to doughnut shops, vaults, and pawn shop backroom entries, you'll uncover these secret locations along Las Vegas Boulevard to Downtown Las Vegas and the local suburban scene. Many of these clandestine locations await unveiling inside the renowned hotels along the Las Vegas Strip.

TIP

Get a complimentary map to explore the array of Las Vegas speakeasies on and off the Strip!

vegasrightnow.com/las-vegas-speakeasies

UNCOVER A SECRET HOTEL

Did you know that Las Vegas is home to ultra-private secret hotels within a hotel? They're not typical boutique hotels (e.g., the notable Cromwell boutique hotel on the Strip). These secret hotel rooms offer the ultimate extravagance and accommodations, such as four-bedroom suites, private pools, backyards, private guest receptions, butler services, Rolls–Royce chauffeured airport transfers, discreet VIP check-ins, and more!

These secret hotels are the perfect choice if you want to indulge in unmatched luxury. What truly sets them apart are their unique experiences and exclusive amenities like privacy, extravagance, and speedy service. It's the epitome of luxe convenience, offering everything only Vegas can provide. These mystical properties hide in plain sight along the famous Las Vegas Strip, nestled inside well-known hotels like Resorts World and MGM Grand. Las Vegas is a dynamic and ever-evolving destination, and these secret hotels are just another unique and intriguing part of the Vegas experience.

TIP

Get a complimentary list to unlock the hidden hotels of Las Vegas!

vegasrightnow.com/las-vegas-secret-hotels

PREPARE
TO ESCAPE IT

Escape IT is a highly rated top destination for those seeking the best escape rooms in Las Vegas. Spanning more than 30,000 square feet, it's a revolutionary new take on traditional escape rooms. Unlike a typical experience, Escape IT is a horror-based, thrill-seeking adventure, offering multiple challenges based on the iconic supernatural horror movie *IT Chapter One* and *IT Chapter Two*.

This escape room is themed with replicas of movie scenes where you try to escape the evil clutches of the terrifying Pennywise the Dancing Clown through mind-bending puzzles and adventures. It's an engaging and exhilarating group activity that will keep you on your toes! Although this escape room is the perfect destination for Halloween-themed activities in Vegas in October, due to its scary nature, it's not recommended for children under 16 unless accompanied by a supervising adult.

273 S M.L.K. Blvd., 702-333-0770
escapeit.com

TIP

Entry to this popular Vegas attraction is by reservation only, and it often sells out weeks ahead. This escape room is especially favored as Halloween approaches in the fall.

EXPERIENCE THE ALLURE
OF A MAGIC SHOW

"No one thinks Las Vegas is real; it is an illusion, but visitors willingly suspend disbelief and pretend."

—UNLV professor Hal Rothman

Las Vegas thrives on spellbinding audiences. And since no one believes the experiences here are real, Vegas is the perfect epicenter for magic shows!

It's been said that "Vegas isn't a city. It's its own magical world." So whether in intimate venues or grand theaters, Las Vegas offers plenty of performances. Legendary magicians like Penn and Teller, David Copperfield, Criss Angel, David Blaine, and Shin Lim have become household names, drawing crowds from around the globe. Additionally, the *Magician's Study* show has gained recognition as a rising star in the city, receiving *Travel + Leisure* and *Forbes* accolades. Each magician conjures their unique combination of illusion, comedy, and wonder, ensuring that there is something mystical for everyone, from grand illusions to intimate up-close mysteries.

SOME OF VEGAS'S MANY INCREDIBLE MAGIC SHOWS

Penn & Teller
Inside Rio Hotel & Casino, 3700 W Flamingo Rd.
pennandteller.com

David Copperfield
Inside MGM Grand, 3799 S Las Vegas Blvd.
davidcopperfield.com

Criss Angel
Inside Planet Hollywood Las Vegas Resort & Casino
3667 Las Vegas Blvd. S
crissangel.com

David Blaine
At Wynn, 3131 Las Vegas Blvd. S
davidblaine.com

Shin Lim
At the Venetian, 3355 S Las Vegas Blvd.
shinlimmagic.com

The Magician's Study
*A secret location in Las Vegas
themagiciansstudy.com

The Magician's Study show is not just a performance. It's an immersive experience. Hosted at a secret location only revealed on the day of the show, this interactive performance keeps the audience on their toes! Returning guests are in for an unpredictable surprise, as their previous visit's entry location may differ. The audience plays a crucial role in the show, as the Magician is known for breaking the fourth wall and engaging directly with his guests.

CATCH A MUST-SEE
CIRQUE DU SOLEIL SHOW

As a longtime Vegas traveler turned local, I confidently say that Cirque du Soleil shows are a must-see! I've had the pleasure of seeing all of them, some multiple times, and they are always spectacular.

Why are the Cirque shows a must-see? Each show presents a different story and theme. Yet, every show is an immersive journey brought to life through a blend of exceptional acrobatic performances, captivating theatrical storytelling, and cutting-edge production technology. The sheer artistry and innovation on display set these shows apart from other entertainment offerings in Las Vegas, placing Cirque as a pinnacle of live entertainment.

Witnessing the display of human ability and creativity up close underscores the unique value of these performances. With such a diverse range of shows, your only dilemma will be choosing which one to see first.

cirquedusoleil.com/las-vegas-shows

TIP

The celebrated *Beatles LOVE* show bid farewell in 2024, marking the end of an era for Cirque du Soleil in Las Vegas. However, this closure opens doors to new possibilities for Cirque on the Las Vegas Strip. We can't wait to see what's next!

CIRQUE DU SOLEIL SHOWS

Mystère
Mystère is a show featuring colorful costumes and playful audience interactions where imagination meets high-flying acrobatics.

"O"
"O" is a mesmerizing aquatic show that enchants with its remarkable dive into theatrical innovation. (*"O"* is a wordplay on the French word for water, *eau.*)

KÀ
KÀ is an action-packed show for martial arts enthusiasts. It features a gravity-defying production with a moving stage and sets.

Michael Jackson ONE
Michael Jackson ONE offers an immersive journey through the music of the King of Pop, filled with "wow" moments and breathtaking movements.

Mad Apple
Mad Apple combines adult-themed laugh-out-loud comedy with magic and classic Cirque stories told through mind-blowing acrobatic feats.

WATCH THE FOURTH OF JULY
FIREWORKS DISPLAY

Every year, on the Fourth of July, various locations offer spectacular views of the fireworks shows that embody the patriotic spirit of Las Vegas. Notably, the Las Vegas Strip, Fremont Street, and suburbia's Downtown Summerlin area become focal points of festivity, with the sky above them lit in explosive wonder!

Inspired by the fireworks shows at Disneyland, families and friends can gather on the Strip for shows at Caesars Palace, Downtown Las Vegas at the Plaza Hotel, or Summerlin Las Vegas at the Red Rock Casino Resort & Spa. Each location promises a unique experience with distinct celebrations because Vegas does not hold back on Independence Day!

Caesars Palace
3570 S Las Vegas Blvd.

Plaza Hotel & Casino
1 N Main St.

Red Rock Casino Resort & Spa
11011 W Charleston Blvd.

TIP

While the fireworks are a sight to behold from almost anywhere in Downtown Las Vegas or on the Strip, local wisdom dictates that the best views of Vegas fireworks are from the hotel parking garage, restaurant rooftop, or adult swim pool viewing parties.

ELEVATE YOUR VEGAS EXPERIENCE
ON THE HIGH ROLLER

It's never been easier to enjoy incredible panoramic views of the Strip and the surrounding Vegas Valley. At a towering 550 feet, the High Roller holds the title of the world's tallest observation wheel, a highlight in the Las Vegas skyline. This unforgettable ride offers a one-of-a-kind perspective on the city's glittering expanse. Overlook the sunlight reflecting off the city's shiny hotel towers adjacent to sparkling pool waters during the day, and at night, enjoy the Strip's neon-lit show. You'll find an adrenaline rush looking over this great city at a height higher than the *Statue of Liberty*—the actual one in New York and the replica in Vegas!

3535 Las Vegas Blvd. S, 855-234-7469
caesars.com/linq/things-to-do/attractions/high-roller

TIP

For more panoramic views, consider adding the STRAT Hotel's Observation Deck and the 360-degree rotating dining room of Top of the World restaurant. The Observation Deck is the tallest freestanding observation tower in the US at an astounding 1,149 feet!

2000 Las Vegas Blvd. S, thestrat.com

Red Rock Canyon

SPORTS
AND RECREATION

UNLOCK EXCLUSIVE ACCESS
TO THE LAS VEGAS RAIDERS

Allegiant Stadium is a modern-day arena marvel and a source of pride for the Las Vegas Raiders and their fans. During football season, you can witness the Raiders play at their state-of-the-art home field adjacent to the Las Vegas Strip. Year-round, Allegiant Stadium tours provide exclusive access to the team's sacred spaces, making you feel like an official part of the Raiders family.

As a guest, you'll receive an all-access pass to explore hidden gems of the stadium, including the private suites, the Broadcast Booth, players' and Raiderettes' locker rooms, and the celebrated Al Davis Memorial Torch. You'll even have the chance to walk through the Wynn Field Club, a premier nightclub that spans the entire length of the north end zone and boasts a $100K club admission! But the tour doesn't end there. It also provides a rare and exclusive opportunity to set foot on the hallowed field, a dream come true for many fans!

3333 Al Davis Way, 1-800-RAIDERS
allegiantstadium.com

TIP

Enhance your guided tour experience by opting for the family-friendly VIP drinks and snacks at the end.

SEE THE THRILLING ASCENT
OF THE LAS VEGAS ACES

The Las Vegas Aces have become a prominent force in the WNBA and a cornerstone of Las Vegas sports. From their early years to clinching back-to-back championships, their journey has been a master class in excellence! Witness Aces players shatter records at any of their home games at Michelob ULTRA Arena, affectionally called "The House," inside Mandalay Bay Resort and Casino. The future shines brightly for this championship team, not just in their own achievements but also in their role as inspiration for the next generation of WNBA athletes and the future of women's professional sports.

If you're in town in September or October and the Aces are in the WNBA Finals, don't miss the chance to get tickets. Experience some of the most exhilarating games!

3950 S Las Vegas Blvd.
aces.wnba.com

TIP

Get your tickets early because the Las Vegas Aces are beloved in their city, and season tickets often sell out quickly! Still, if you're in town, check ticket outlets for any available resale tickets. Then, prepare your winning defense chant for game day: "You can't win in this House!"

WITNESS UNLV
FAN CULTURE

The UNLV Rebels have always been a beacon for exceptional talent in Las Vegas sports, particularly college basketball and football. Their journey through NCAA competitions has showcased the prowess of athletes and the strategic minds of the coaching staff, a group that commands respect and admiration. But it's not just about the games. Unique traditions and community engagements, like pregame festivities and rallies, truly bond Rebels fans and make you feel like an integral part of Nevada's sports culture.

For Rebels football fans, the thrill of game days at the city's state-of-the-art Allegiant Stadium is an experience like no other. The energy, the anticipation, and the sheer excitement of the game are palpable. Meanwhile, the Runnin' Rebels men's and Lady Rebels women's basketball teams play on campus at their gigantic arenas, offering equally thrilling experiences.

UNLV Runnin' Rebels men's basketball
Thomas & Mack Center, 4505 S Maryland Pkwy.
unlvrebels.com/sports/mens-basketball

UNLV Lady Rebels women's basketball
Cox Pavilion, 4505 S Maryland Pkwy., #2022
unlvrebels.com/sports/womens-basketball

UNLV Rebels football
Allegiant Stadium, 3333 Al Davis Way
unlvrebels.com/sports/football

WATCH
THE VEGAS GOLDEN KNIGHTS ON ICE

Securing the championship Stanley Cup and the NHL's Stanley Award for Game Presentation three times was no small feat for the Vegas Golden Knights. Battle born in Vegas, the team has an unparalleled commitment to delivering breathtaking on-ice entertainment by combining state-of-the-art technology with electrifying performances rooted in Las Vegas showmanship. This has set a new standard in ice sports, deepening fan loyalty and turning game nights into unforgettable experiences.

When in town during hockey season, check local bars and eateries up, down, and off the Strip advertising Golden Knights watch-party nights. This team is Vegas royalty, so you may find yourself in the right place at the right time for the cherished season kickoff events and fanfare player meet and greets within the Las Vegas community.

T-Mobile Arena
3780 S Las Vegas Blvd.
nhl.com/goldenknights

TIP

Look for the Vegas Golden Knights on and off the ice when you're in town. The team has extended its reach beyond its T-Mobile Arena home, actively participating in community initiatives. Notably, making significant contributions during Black History Month and military and first responders appreciation events, inspiring and making us all proud.

TAKE ME OUT
TO THE BALL GAME

The Las Vegas Ballpark, home to the Las Vegas Aviators, a Triple-A Affiliate of the Oakland A's (soon to be the Las Vegas A's), offers a unique baseball venue. With seating options ranging from the exclusive Club Level suites to the cozy General Admission Berm/Social section, there's something for every fan.

Its All-Inclusive Food + Beverage section is a haven for fans who value convenience and variety. From classic ballpark snacks to gourmet dishes, there's something to satisfy your every craving. Additionally, unique experiences are waiting at the Party Deck and the splash-ready Outfield Pool (yes, there's even a pool!). These special sections are designed to pique your interest and add a touch of excitement to your visit, reflecting the ballpark's commitment to an only-in-Vegas fan experience!

1650 S Pavilion Center Dr.
thelvballpark.com

TIP

Each holiday season, the ballpark transforms into Enchant, the world's largest Christmas light maze adventure. With unique ice-skating and countless other festive attractions, it's a magical experience not to be missed!

enchantchristmas.com/city/las-vegas-nv-ballpark

SADDLE UP
FOR EXCITEMENT AT THE HELLDORADO DAYS RODEO

Get ready for an exciting experience at the Helldorado Days Rodeo! This event celebrates rodeo events and cowboy culture, honoring the history of Las Vegas. The rodeo takes place at the unique CORE Arena in Downtown Las Vegas, the city's first permanent outdoor equestrian center. It's located next to the Plaza Hotel & Casino, with 80 stalls available for year-round use, making it convenient for equestrians to "kiss their horses goodnight" and be assured that their animals will be safe.

At Helldorado, you can expect a range of traditional rodeo competitions, such as bull riding, barrel racing, and steer wrestling, all set in a family-friendly atmosphere. The location even features two outdoor arenas for roping practice and exercise during the rodeo event. Helldorado Days Rodeo is a chance to see cowhand champions in action, enjoy laughter under cowboy hats, and watch children interacting with rodeo clowns while celebrating the rancher spirit against the vibrant western backdrop of Las Vegas.

324 S Main St.
plazahotelcasino.com/entertainment/helldorado-days-rodeo

WATCH A GAME
AT THE LARGEST
SPORTSBOOK IN THE WORLD

Circa Resort & Casino in Downtown Las Vegas boasts the largest seating capacity and a 78-million-pixel screen, making it the world's largest sportsbook and the ultimate destination for sports enthusiasts! It's a contemporary, three-story sports betting space in the heart of Las Vegas's Fremont Street Experience. It offers abundant modern-day hotel amenities and a touch of old-fashioned Vegas hospitality.

Circa is the newest hotel in Downtown Las Vegas, making a splash on the DTLV scene! If you're booking a stay for the summer months, you're in for a treat with their super popular All-In Summer Hotel Package. This hotel special has been an annual hit that beats the Vegas heat with a two-night stay, restaurant dining credit, separate beverage credit, and a coveted daybed at Circa's exclusive amphitheater-style pool, Stadium Swim—the best outdoor venue to watch your favorite sports.

8 Fremont St., 702-247-2258
circalasvegas.com

TIP
Circa Resort & Casino is an exclusive, adults-only 21+ property, providing a distinctive and sophisticated experience for you to take a break from adulting!

SWING THROUGH SIN CITY
AT PREMIER GOLF CLUBS

Amid its vast desert landscape, luxury golf in Las Vegas thrives, offering you premier golf experiences on lush, meticulously designed courses. The Strip boasts exclusive golf rates at championship golf courses like the prestigious Wynn Golf Club, reimagined by Tom Fazio golf design. The more than 20 golf resorts in the Las Vegas Valley create an all-in-one luxury vacation experience.

Two great Vegas golf clubs to visit:

Wynn Golf Club
3131 Las Vegas Blvd. S
702-770-4653
wynnlasvegas.com/experiences/golf

Bali Hai Golf Club
5160 S Las Vegas Blvd.
702-597-2400
balihaigolfclub.com

TIP

For family-fun, try out a high-tech driving range!

Topgolf at MGM Grand
4627 Koval Ln., 702-933-8458, topgolf.com/us/las-vegas

Five Iron Golf at AREA15
3215 S Rancho Dr., #250, 800-513-5153, fiveirongolf.com/locations/las-vegas-area15

Atomic Golf
1850 S Main St., 702-819-7429, atomicgolf.com

ZIP-LINE THROUGH
AN EXPERIENCE THAT DOES NOT EXIST

AREA15 is an immersive entertainment complex in the heart of Las Vegas, just a mile from the famous Strip. It offers various experiences, including interactive museums, entertainment attractions, AI games, restaurants, bars, and nightlife, all within a colossal warehouse with an outside campus. Its name is a play on the name of the mysterious and conspiracy-theoried government test and training area in Nevada, Area 51. The hub's tagline is "This experience does not exist!"

One of its standout attractions is the zip line Haley's Comet, which promises an exciting adrenaline rush. It offers a unique view of this otherworldly venue, providing a bird's-eye perspective of the retro-futuristic space.

3215 S Rancho Dr.
area15.com

TIP

Another famous zip line in Vegas is SlotZilla, a 77-feet-high slot machine–inspired attraction at Downtown Las Vegas's Fremont Street Experience. SlotZilla offers two thrilling rides under its massive outdoor canopy: the lower Zipline and the upper Zoomline.

SlotZilla
425 Fremont St., #160, 702-678-5780
vegasexperience.com/slotzilla-zip-line

REV UP
FOR THE LAS VEGAS GRAND PRIX

The Las Vegas Grand Prix is not your typical motorsport event. In Vegas, it's the biggest race of the year and part of the Formula 1 (F1) World Championship, combining high speed and the vibrant allure of the Entertainment Capital of the World! This extraordinary event transforms the famous Las Vegas Strip into the Las Vegas Strip Circuit, a high-speed racing paradise, unlike any other location on the F1 calendar! The city's unique blend of dazzling nightlife and iconic attractions provides a spectacular backdrop, promising an electric atmosphere illuminated via a skyline exclusive to Las Vegas.

4400 Koval Ln., f1lasvegasgp.com

TIP

Check out the Grand Prix Racing Sim at AREA15, a mile off the Strip, and enjoy an interactive simulated video game of the Las Vegas racing circuit. Or, just 15 minutes from the Strip, check out the Las Vegas Mini Grand Prix—an amusement park, arcade, and go-kart speedway.

Grand Prix Racing Sim	Las Vegas Mini Grand Prix
Inside AREA15, 3215 S Rancho Dr.	1401 N Rainbow Blvd.
area15.com/experiences/grand-prix-racing	lvmgp.com

EXPERIENCE
SKY-HIGH EXCITEMENT
AT AVIATION NATION

Experience thrilling aerial performances at the Nellis Air Force Base Air Show. This event, known as "Aviation Nation," takes place on the military base eight miles northeast of Downtown Las Vegas. The air show showcases aviation history through dynamic aerial demonstrations and static aircraft displays like remotely piloted aircraft systems and fighter aircraft. You can witness various breathtaking aerobatic performances, like nimble fighter jets executing tight turns, rolls, and dives.

Nellis is home to the United States Air Force air demonstration squadron, the Thunderbirds. They are the world's third-oldest formal flying aerobatic team under the same name. The Thunderbirds Squadron travels across the United States and worldwide, showcasing aerobatic formation and solo flying in specially marked aircraft. They are the featured performers at the annual air show above their home base in Las Vegas.

nellis.af.mil/Aviation-Nation

TIP

The best part about Aviation Nation is that the air show is free and open to the public—no military ID is even needed.

SOAR ABOVE SIN CITY
ON A HELICOPTER TOUR

Las Vegas helicopter tours are adventure tourism at its finest! With Whisper Jet technology to provide a quiet ride, forward-facing seats, and large sightseeing windows, you'll experience a comfortable ride with safety as the top priority. As you soar above the city's famous casinos and resorts, you'll discover that Las Vegas helicopter tours offer a secure and unique experience, not just a bucket list idea.

If you're a thrill seeker or crave extreme adventure, the helicopters can fly your tour with the doors off!

This is a partial list selection of the city's numerous helicopter tours.

Maverick Helicopters
702-430-7583
maverickhelicopter.com

Skyline Helicopter Tours (doors-off tours)
702-382-8687
skylinehelicoptertours.com

TIP

Channel your inner Top Gun Maverick in a real-life fighter pilot experience and play stunt pilot for a day. This rare, in-air adventure includes a sky combat experience and advanced plane aerobatics. And the best part? You get to fly the plane—with an in-flight pilot guiding you every step of the way.

Sky Combat Ace
888-494-5850, skycombatace.com

FLIP THROUGH HISTORY
AT THE PINBALL HALL OF FAME

Welcome to the Pinball Hall of Fame, where you can experience the thrill of playing the cheapest slots on the Strip. But these are no ordinary slots. There are no prizes or arcade-style ticket redemptions. It's all about pure pinball here, with a few novelty arcade games thrown in. With pinball machines from the 1950s to the 1990s, the Hall of Fame is an interactive journey through pinball history showcasing an expansive range of games you can play. And with over 25,000 square feet of gaming space, it's an attempt at the world's most expansive pinball collection!

At the Pinball Hall of Fame, you'll find everything from the earliest coin-operated machines to the latest pinball gaming. This diversity not only captivates but also educates, charting the evolution of arcade games. Every flip helps preserve the pinball tradition, adding a touch of nostalgia to Las Vegas's gaming scene. And since it's a nonprofit, the hall focuses on providing a simple, enjoyable gaming experience.

4925 Las Vegas Blvd. S
702-597-2627, pinballmuseum.org

TIP
Entrance is free but bring quarters for the coin-operated machines that support this nonprofit's mission of preserving the world's largest pinball collection!

CHASE YOUR TRAVEL WHIMS
AT SEVEN MAGIC MOUNTAINS

Las Vegas is renowned for its immersive art installations, but Seven Magic Mountains stands out as a truly unique attraction. This striking public installation features seven towering structures, each over 30 feet tall, made of vibrant, rainbow-painted boulders sourced locally. It's a must-see, especially for art enthusiasts and wanderlust-struck travelers alike.

The artwork will not only captivate you as it has so many Instagram audiences and social media followers—#SevenMagicMountains. But it also draws visitors from all over the globe, creating a sense of global community around this whimsical natural attraction in Las Vegas.

Free parking lot at the installation
S Las Vegas Blvd.
sevenmagicmountains.com

TIP

While this mountainous artwork is big, bold, and breathtaking, it's important to note that Seven Magic Mountains is only accessible during daylight hours. Unlike the neon-lit Las Vegas Strip, it features no artificial lights, creating an intriguing contrast with the natural desert setting.

ESCAPE TO A DESERT OASIS
AT SPRINGS PRESERVE

Las Vegas holds a unique treasure and escape called Springs Preserve. This urban oasis, just a short drive from the city's bustle, is known as the birthplace of Las Vegas. It celebrates the beauty of desert life, landscaping, and the importance of conservation. This 180-acre desert oasis features many attractions, including museums, a botanical garden, an animal habitat, an interactive historical streetscape, a train ride, live shows, classes, seasonal festivals, and more! Springs Preserve is a thrilling showcase of the history of Las Vegas and a vital guardian of the Mojave Desert's diverse ecosystems.

If you're fortunate enough to visit Springs Preserve in October or November, take advantage of the garden's Butterfly Habitat, Haunted Harvest, and Dia de Muertos, the city's largest cultural Day of the Dead event, all happening during the season of Vegas's best weather.

333 S Valley View Blvd., 702-822-7700,
springspreserve.org

SOME SUGGESTED ITINERARIES

Visiting for an hour or two?

The Origen Museum
Traveling exhibit (changes throughout the year)
Miracle in the Mojave film
Flash flood exhibit
Animal habitat

Visiting for half a day?

Enjoy the above attractions plus. . .

Botanical garden
Boomtown 1905
WaterWorks
Butterfly habitat (seasonal)
Sustainability Gallery & Nature Exchange
DesertSol

Visiting for a full day?

Enjoy the above attractions plus. . .

Nevada State Museum
Art exhibits inside the Primrose Gallery
Trails and train rides
Playground and splash pad
Gift shop
Springs Cafe

UNCOVER THE VEGAS VALLEY'S
NATURAL GEMS

Red Rock Canyon National Conservation Area

Red Rock Canyon, a mere 25-minute drive from the Las Vegas Strip, is a geological wonderland with breathtaking rock formations and scenic beauty. The visitor center offers educational programs that shed light on the vibrant red and rust-colored rock hills and canyons, with the Spring Mountains as its painted backdrop. This enriching experience adds an intellectual dimension to your outdoor adventure.

702-515-5350
redrockcanyonlv.org

TIP

Entrance fees vary by location and guided tour. Some companies offer day trips to multiple areas and even provide transportation from the Las Vegas Strip. You can opt for a comfortable shuttle bus tour with plenty of scenic stops or live it up on an adventurous motor scooter tour!

Red Rock Discovery Tours
702-956-4140, redrockdiscoverytours.com

Mount Charleston

Head west of the Las Vegas Valley to the Spring Mountains, where Charleston Peak (Mount Charleston) reaches almost 12,000 feet! Just 35 miles from Downtown Las Vegas, this area offers year-round winter sports and a haven for cabins and ski lodges. Its dense forests and high altitudes provide a refreshing escape from nearby Vegas's intense summer heat, drawing hikers and campers to its serene, snow-capped mountainous landscapes. In the winter, the majestic mountain becomes a playground for you if you're a skier or a white Christmas enthusiast.

702-872-5486
gomtcharleston.com

Spring Mountain Ranch State Park

Nestled beside Red Rock Canyon, Spring Mountain Ranch holds rich historical significance. Once a luxurious retreat owned by luminaries such as Las Vegas real estate developer and once the wealthiest man in the world, Howard Hughes, and celebrity socialite Vera Krupp, this Nevada state park offers more than scenic views and tranquil hiking trails. You can explore archaeological sites and the storied ranch house and observe wildlife, including wild burros. Picture multiple donkeys from *Shrek*. Guided tours unveil a natural journey through time and bring the park's history to life. With a bonus stop at the quaint town of Blue Diamond, Spring Mountain Ranch is a must-see for so many reasons.

6375 Hwy. 159, Blue Diamond, 702-875-4141
parks.nv.gov/parks/spring-mountain-ranch

TOUR NEVADA'S
OLDEST STATE PARK

Valley of Fire State Park is a living museum of natural history and a great place to visit, only 45 minutes from Las Vegas. This desert oasis covers 46,000 acres, and it's Nevada's oldest and largest state park, featuring a stunning landscape of fiery red Aztec sandstone. This unique geological marvel was formed over 150 million years ago by shifting sand dunes that left multicolored streaks in the rocks. Officially becoming a state park in 1934, it's also home to ancient petroglyphs dating back over 2,000 years. You'll enjoy camping, hiking scenic trails, and learning about prehistory at the park's visitor center amid this breathtaking red landscape.

Overton
702-397-2088
parks.nv.gov/parks/valley-of-fire

TIP

Valley of Fire State Park is conveniently located just 2.5 hours from Zion National Park, Utah's first national park. The well-marked roads make it an easy and enjoyable drive, perfect for a fun day trip! Both parks are recognized in their states as Mojave Desert nature preserve firsts, known for their vibrant red hues. While Zion Canyon features steep red cliffs, Valley of Fire showcases a stunning red landscape of sandstone and natural rock, particularly beautiful at sunset.

Zion National Park, Utah, 435-772-3256, nps.gov/zion

FIND A NATIONAL PARK

A national park is a designated nature preserve owned by the government for conservation purposes. Explore three national parks less than an hour from Las Vegas. You can even book guided tour experiences departing from the Strip!

Lake Mead National Recreation Area is a reservoir formed by the Hoover Dam, creating an array of marinas, lakes, and even a beach. In contrast, Tule Springs Fossil Beds is a natural landscape forming the upper Las Vegas Valley, preserving Ice Age fossil discoveries along natural hiking trails, while the Mojave National Preserve boasts mountainous valleys and sand dunes for days.

Just over two hours away are Zion and Death Valley. Both offer diverse desert landscapes, from Zion's red and pink sandstone cliffs to Death Valley, the country's hottest, driest, and lowest elevation with its unique areas of arid, white, salt-covered grounds. The Grand Canyon is about four hours away if you're up for a half-day drive. It's one of the world's seven natural wonders, showcasing side-by-side million-year-old and billion-year-old rocks with one unanswered question in the middle—what happened during the years in between?

Lake Mead
National Recreation Area
702-293-8990, nps.gov/lake

Tule Springs Fossil
Beds National Monument
702-293-8853, nps.gov/tusk

Zion National Park
435-772-3256, nps.gov/zion

Death Valley National Park
760-786-3200, nps.gov/deva

Mojave National Preserve
760-252-6100, nps.gov/moja

Grand Canyon National Park
928-638-7779, nps.gov/grca

GET TO KNOW
THE GREEN SIDE OF VEGAS

As entertaining as Las Vegas can be, there's even more to discover beyond the famous Strip! The city holds a lesser-known treasure trove of green spaces and recreational opportunities. Parks in Las Vegas present a peaceful contrast to the city's lively urban ambiance, offering a refreshing escape. These areas showcase an unexpected side of the city, where nature thrives. On your next visit, consider taking a break from the Strip's attractions to explore Las Vegas's outdoor fun, from picturesque dog parks to engaging, family-friendly natural environments like Lorenzi Park, Floyd Lamb Park, Clark County Wetlands Park, or Ice Age Fossils State Park.

Lorenzi Park
3333 W Washington Ave., 702-229-7529
lasvegasnevada.gov/residents/parks-facilities/lorenzi-park

Floyd Lamb Park
9200 Tule Springs Rd., 702-229-8100
lasvegasnevada.gov/residents/parks-facilities/floyd-lamb-park

Clark County Wetlands Park
7050 Wetlands Park Ln., 702-455-7522
clarkcountynv.gov/government/departments/
parks___recreation/wetlands_park

Ice Age Fossils State Park
8660 N Decatur Blvd., North Las Vegas, 702-478-9300
parks.nv.gov/parks/ice-age-fossils

TIP

You'll find plenty of fresh air and natural adventure in Las Vegas but fewer grassy green spaces. The city gets less than 30 days of rain yearly, so it's committed to conserving water. As part of its sustainability efforts, nonrecreational grass that requires a lot of watering is being replaced with rock garden desert landscaping. This change helps prevent water from being absorbed into the ground just to maintain aesthetics, as that water cannot be recycled or preserved.

SPOT A FLAMINGO
ON THE STRIP

The Flamingo Wildlife Habitat is an unexpected gem that offers a peaceful escape in the heart of the Las Vegas Strip. This wildlife sanctuary and tropical oasis is nestled in the lush gardens of the Flamingo Las Vegas Hotel & Casino. The bright pink flamingos immediately catch your eye in this natural retreat, where they coexist with various wildlife, including graceful koi fish, serene turtles, and exotic birds whose songs fill the air. This eco-friendly habitat and experience includes educational animal keeper talks, nature photography opportunities, and moments of contemplation amid waterfalls and wandering streams. Best of all, it's a family-friendly environment right on the famous Strip, with no reservations required and no entry fee.

3555 Las Vegas Blvd. S, 702-733-3349
caesars.com/flamingo-las-vegas/things-to-do/wildlife-habitat

TIP

Get ready for the 100-acre Las Vegas Zoological Park, a project by the Las Vegas Zoological Society that will be home to more than 900 animals representing 300 species! Keep an eye on the project's progress on their website.

702-217-1869
zoolasvegas.org

In the meantime, you can explore indoor aquariums and petting zoo experiences at SeaQuest. It's a land-and-sea adventure where you can make lifelong connections with wildlife and sea animals.

Inside Boulevard Mall
3528 S Maryland Pkwy., Ste. #340
visitseaquest.com/vegas

SPLASH AROUND
AT CIRCUS CIRCUS

The Adventuredome, located within the timeless Circus Circus Hotel & Casino, is an indoor theme park that operates all year-round. Its amusement park attractions ensure entertainment for every member of your family, from exhilarating roller coasters to energetic arcade games and inviting mini-golf courses.

Circus Circus's Splash Zone & Pool, a kid's water park paradise, shines during the Vegas pool season from March to October. As the only water park on the Las Vegas Strip, it offers an exclusive experience. The Slide Tower, a 50-foot-tall multicolor descent, will immediately captivate your family upon entry. The Splash Pad, with its water cannons, rain tree, and colossal spill bucket, is a water playground that ignites endless imagination. There are also two large pools and whirlpools to enjoy under the Vegas sun!

2880 S Las Vegas Blvd., 702-734-0410
circuscircus.com

TIP

While anyone can pay for admission to the Adventuredome, access to the Splash Zone & Pool is reserved only for registered guests of Circus Circus Hotel. However, staying at the hotel is a smart choice. Considering the room rates are usually under $100 per night, including taxes, it's a cost-effective way for your entire family to enjoy the water park and play all day!

SWIM WITH THE SHARKS
IN THE TANK

For anyone fascinated by Shark Week, marine ecosystems, or looking for a thrilling Las Vegas attraction, the pool at Golden Nugget is an unforgettable dive! The Golden Nugget Hotel & Casino is renowned for its luxurious shark tank pool, known simply as "The Tank." This marvel features an extraordinary shark aquarium and an exhilarating 300-foot waterslide, making it unlike any other. With a $30 million investment backing this 200,000-gallon creation, you can safely slide through the aquarium and see the sharks swimming next to you as you pass through! It's a unique experience that underscores The Tank's exceptional quality, which is part of why the Las Vegas pool scene has set such high standards.

129 Fremont St., 702-385-7111
goldennugget.com/las-vegas/amenities/h2o-pool

TIP

Visit Chart House at the Golden Nugget and enjoy an exclusive view of its 75,000-gallon tropical fish aquarium. You can also download the aquarium guide for an educational journey into the aquatic life of the Chart House fishies beneath the aquarium's waves.

goldennugget.com/las-vegas/restaurants/chart-house

EXPLORE RECREATIONAL FUN
AT A DESERT LAKE

Las Vegas, nestled in the heart of the desert, will surprise you with its unique geography. The city boasts approximately 12 manufactured lakes and reservoirs, starkly contrasting its arid surroundings. These human-created wonders, including Lake Mead and Lake Mohave, owe their existence to the Hoover and Davis Dams. This remarkable landscape transformation has added a distinct aquatic element to the Las Vegas Valley, a sight sure to intrigue you.

From the grandeur of Lake Mead, America's largest reservoir, to the hidden oasis of Lake Sahara within its suburban community, these impressive waterways, a rare find in the desert, are not just for show. They inspire many activities, from swimming and sailing to camping, bird-watching, and picnicking. The excitement of these recreational opportunities will captivate the outdoor enthusiast in you. Be sure to explore other area lakes listed on the facing page.

Lake Mead
Boulder City, 702-293-8990
nps.gov/lake/index.htm

Lake Mohave
Boulder City, Nevada, and Bullhead City, Arizona
702-293-8990
nps.gov/lake/learn/nature/overview-of-lake-mohave.htm

Lake Sahara
The Lakes Community, 702-605-7482
robjensen.com/communities/the-lakes

Desert Shores lakes
(Lake Jacqueline, Lake Sarah,
Lake Maddison, Lake Lindsey)
Desert Shores Community, 702-254-1020
www.mydesertshores.com

Lake Las Vegas
Henderson, 702-568-7948
lakelasvegas.com

Tule Springs Lake
9200 Tule Springs Rd., 702-229-6297
travelnevada.com/parks-recreational-areas/
floyd-lamb-park-at-tule-springs

Aliante Nature Discovery Park
North Las Vegas, 702-267-4000
travelnevada.com/parks-recreational-
areas-aliante-nature-discovery-park

Lorenzi Park
3333 W Washington Ave., 702-229-7529
lasvegasnevada.gov/residents/parks-facilities/lorenzi-park

Cornerstone Park
Henderson, 702-267-4000
travelnevada.com/parks-recreational-areas/cornerstone-park

BASK IN THE SUN
AT A DESERT BEACH

Let me introduce you to another side of Las Vegas—one that tourists rarely get to know. Vegas is not just for gamblers. Activities here cater to all preferences, offering relaxation and even water play! This entertainment oasis is landlocked in the heart of the desert, so natural and ocean beaches are not nearby. However, some Vegas resort properties have created beach-like settings within the Mojave Desert.

Surprisingly, the city also offers diverse beach experiences, from the family-friendly Tahiti Village to the secluded beach clubs tucked away in Vegas's private communities and resorts. There's something naturally special about escaping the neon-lit Strip to relax by the shore at Boulder Beach, the Boulder Basin of Lake Mead. It's worth remembering that sometimes, the real adventure begins where the city lights end!

TIP

Most of the beaches in Las Vegas are private, so you can expect to pay a day fee for entry. Alternatively, you can access them for free with an overnight stay at the hosting property.

VISIT A VEGAS BEACH

Boulder Beach
Lake Mead National Recreation Area, Boulder City
702-293-2540
nps.gov/places/boulder-beach.htm

Desert Shores Lagoon Beach Park
2500 Regatta Dr., 702-254-1020
www.mydesertshores.com

Lake Las Vegas
Henderson, 702-568-7948
lakelasvegas.com

Mandalay Bay Beach at Mandalay Bay Resort and Casino
3950 S Las Vegas Blvd., 877-305-3136
mandalaybay.mgmresorts.com/en/amenities/beach.html

Rio Pool at Rio Hotel & Casino
3700 W Flamingo Rd., 866-746-7671
riolasvegas.com/rio-pool

Sand Entry Pool at Tahiti Village Resort & Spa
7200 S Las Vegas Blvd., 702-440-6800
tahitivillage.com

Green Valley Ranch Pool
2300 Paseo Verde Pkwy., Henderson, 702-617-7777
greenvalleyranch.com/see-and-do/pool

GO TO MERMAID SCHOOL

Live out your Disney princess dreams at Silverton Casino Lodge as part of their Mermaid School. This is more than just an experience. It's a whole lot of fun! You'll start with a behind-the-scenes tour of the 117,000-gallon aquarium to learn about the fish and their care. After the tour, you'll head to the top of the tank for a mermaid training session.

As a member of the mermaid squad, you'll receive a stunning mermaid tail and goggles. Professional photos will capture your transformation, and voila! You're now a mermaid, gracefully swimming in the Silverton Aquarium amid tropical fish and exotic ocean life, and all the casino guests can see you living your best mermaid life! This experience best suits strong swimmers, both kids and adults, and is excellent for small groups and birthday parties.

3333 Blue Diamond Rd., 702-263-7777
silvertoncasino.com/event/mermaid-school

TIP

Don't miss the daily magic of the Silverton Mermaid Swims, voted one of the "Best Free Attractions in Las Vegas." The mermaids swim every half hour in the aquarium Thursday through Sunday, and you can also watch from the Silverton Mermaid Restaurant & Lounge.

ICE-SKATE IN THE DESERT

Las Vegas offers a unique ice-skating experience in a desert setting, with indoor and outdoor rinks. The city becomes a unique and enchanting destination during winter, offering a blend of winter sports and desert warmth. You can take figure skating classes or ice hockey training at the Las Vegas Ice Center or enjoy seasonal outdoor options like the Ice Rink at the Cosmopolitan on the famous Strip and the Rock Rink at Downtown Summerlin.

Imagine the fantasy of ice-skating in front of the stunning backdrop of Red Rock Canyon or the captivating rooftop skating experience overlooking the iconic Vegas skyline under the stars. This unique mix makes ice-skating in Vegas a truly memorable and intriguing experience.

Las Vegas Ice Center
9295 W Flamingo Rd., Unit 130, 702-320-7777
www.lasvegasice.com

The Ice Rink at the Cosmopolitan (seasonal)
3708 Las Vegas Blvd. S, Boulevard Tower, Level 4, 702-698-7475
cosmopolitanlasvegas.mgmresorts.com/en/
entertainment/the-ice-rink

The Rock Rink at Downtown Summerlin (seasonal)
1825 Festival Plaza Dr.
summerlin.com/events

Fontainebleau Oasis Ice Rink
2777 S Las Vgas Blvd.
fontainebleaulasvegas.com/experiences/oasis-ice-rink

CULTURE
AND HISTORY

SEE THE HISTORY
OF LAS VEGAS ILLUMINATED

Located in Downtown Las Vegas, the Neon Museum's mission is to preserve retired neon signs from casinos, businesses, and landmarks. These iconic signs are displayed in the outdoor museum space known as the Neon Boneyard and continue to tell the dazzling stories of vintage Las Vegas through their massive size, vibrant colors, and brightly lit bulbs, offering a unique visual storytelling experience that's intrinsic to today's selfie culture.

Open 365 days a year, daytime and evening admission is available. Explore at your own pace, take a guided tour, or have an immersive experience in augmented reality! Las Vegas locals can use their library cards to check out a Family Pass for free admission to STEAM Saturdays, a program focusing on science, technology, engineering, art, and math.

The museum actively collects photos and artifacts from visitors, creating an archive of vintage Vegas. They also have a program called RACHEL (Record and Collect Historical Experiences in Las Vegas), which allows you to record and share your personal Vegas stories. Visit RACHEL in the museum store.

Be sure to also visit The Mob Museum at 300 Stewart Ave. (themobmuseum.org), Las Vegas National History Museum at 900 Las Vegas Blvd. N (lvnhm.org), and Zak Bagans' The Haunted Museum at 600 E Charleston Blvd. (thehauntedmuseum.com).

770 Las Vegas Blvd. N, 702-387-6366
neonmuseum.org

CREATE AN INSTAGRAM STORY
AT THE LAS VEGAS SIGN

What's that saying? "It ain't real until you post it!" Then you want to make it official with a visit to the Welcome to Fabulous Las Vegas Sign when you arrive in Sin City! This free attraction embodies the city's spirit, immersing you in Las Vegas history and ensuring an unforgettable trip. The allure of snapping a photo, sharing that moment, and knowing you've stood at the gateway to iconic Vegas experiences is a social media dream!

Many replicas of the Welcome to Fabulous Las Vegas Sign exist at hotels and shops along the Strip. However, the original sign is a unique and special landmark just past the Mandalay Bay Resort and Casino at the south end of the famous Strip.

5100 Las Vegas Blvd. S
vegasrightnow.com/is-the-las-vegas-sign-free

TIP

It's free to park and snap pics at the Las Vegas Sign, 24 hours a day! The best times to visit are early morning or late in the day to get the best light and try to avoid crowds. Sunrise, sunset, and the golden hour provide stunning photo opportunities, and you can capture impressive selfies from all angles of the sign.

GET INTRODUCED
TO REIKI AND RARE BOOK COLLECTING

Bauman Rare Books inside the Venetian Resort on the Las Vegas Strip offers an impressive range of rare and antique books, including first editions and signed copies. In the rare edition book world, Bauman attracts bookworms from around the globe seeking to add unique pieces to their collections. You'll see books penned by legendary authors and older works predating the 19th century. Even if you're not a book collector, you'll be captivated by the store's sophisticated ambiance, rich dark wood decor, and warmly lit library aesthetics.

Consider exploring Psychic Eye Book Shops for a different kind of bookstore experience. Their holistic, metaphysical, and spiritual shops are a true treasure trove, offering books and unique items such as candles, incense, herbs, psychic readings, and astrology services.

Bauman Rare Books
3327 Las Vegas Blvd. S, Ste. 2856
702-948-1617
baumanrarebooks.com

Psychic Eye Book Shops
6848 W Charleston Blvd.
702-255-4477
pebooksandgifts.com

TIP

Reiki is a popular relaxation method in Las Vegas. Gayla Malcolm is a well-known practitioner in the city. After a reiki-centering session is the perfect time to pause and discover a new book!

Gayla Malcolm Reikiology, 702-528-5602, gaylamalcolm.com

STARGAZE AT VEGAS'S NORTH STAR,
THE STRATOSPHERE

Standing out in the Vegas skyline, the STRAT (formerly the Stratosphere) is a unique fixture that marks the beginning and end of the Las Vegas Strip. This iconic landmark, visible from almost anywhere in the city, is home to the tallest freestanding observation tower in the US, standing at 1,149 feet! It's a sight to behold, standing tall in the city's skyline like a guiding north star, and a must-visit in Las Vegas.

The STRAT offers various hotel and resort amenities, including a vast casino, restaurants, shopping, a comedy club, a rooftop pool, and modern golf. The top of the tower features a revolving restaurant named Top of the World, the STRAT Observation Deck, and thrill rides including Big Shot and X-Scream. Despite offering resort-style theme park amenities, the STRAT remains accessible, targeting value-conscious visitors with standard rooms and suites. This means you can enjoy the conveniences of a high-end hotel without breaking the bank!

2000 Las Vegas Blvd. S, 800-998-6937
thestrat.com

READ THE CITY'S NEWSPAPERS

Newspapers evoke a feeling of nostalgia, trustworthiness, and a sense of community and belonging. In Las Vegas, the two dedicated newspapers, the *Las Vegas Sun* and the *Las Vegas Review-Journal*, play a crucial role in preserving the city's history. Established over 100 years ago, the *Review-Journal*, formally the *Clark County Review*, is a daily subscription newspaper and the largest circulating daily paper in the state. It is headquartered in Las Vegas.

Both the *Sun* and the *Review-Journal* are mainstays among media outlets in the city. They are known for their commitment to Las Vegas news and investigative journalism, covering everything from politics to sports, weather, and community events such as local conventions and breaking news. Today, these publications embrace both printed papers and digital news, providing a convenient and comfortable way to stay updated with the latest happenings in the city.

Las Vegas Review-Journal
reviewjournal.com

Las Vegas Sun
lasvegassun.com

EMBARK ON A SCAVENGER HUNT
FOR SMALL TREASURES

Step into a unique blend of gallery, archive, and studio at the Office of Collecting & Design. The artist and filmmaker behind this nuanced space has reimagined the traditional role of a collector, as exhibited in this prop library museum.

Delve into an unbridled accumulation of a collection of collections "devoted to the diminutive, the discarded, the misplaced, the broken, and the obsolete!" Scavenge for objects in the museum's collections using a hand-drawn map or curate an impressive, visually appealing arrangement of objects. Make a flat lay that's Instagram-worthy and arranged from an eclectic display of tiny treasures. You'll leave feeling engaged and aesthetically satisfied in this bizarre yet beautiful place!

702-613-8571
officeofcollecting.com

TIP

The Office of Collecting & Design is hitting the road and transforming into the traveling museum of your dreams. Even on wheels, you can still open every drawer, explore every box, and discover to your heart's content! Check their website for updates on this mobile museum experience. Due to the delicate nature of the tiny artifacts, this museum is not recommended for children.

RELIVE THE BLOCKBUSTER
OPPENHEIMER IN REAL LIFE

If you're not a science buff, you'll become one after visiting the National Atomic Testing Museum in Las Vegas! Explore a treasured gallery with interactive exhibits and engaging presentations that bring the story of the Atomic Age to life. You'll be captivated by the timeline of the Hollywood blockbuster *Oppenheimer* as you immerse yourself in a world of nuclear science and history. (Oppenheimer's granddaughter currently lives in Southern Nevada!)

The Atomic Museum focuses on the first above-ground nuclear testing conducted only 70 miles north of Las Vegas in 1951 and its catastrophic effects over the following 40 years. The museum is dedicated to informing and educating visitors about its impact. It also features an expanded exhibit about the secretive and highly classified Area 51, the United States Air Force facility within the Nevada Test and Training Range. Not to be confused with AREA15 in Las Vegas, an extraordinary and immersive entertainment complex.

755 E Flamingo Rd., 702-409-7366
atomicmuseum.vegas

TIP
Make time to visit the museum's gift shop, which offers quirky souvenirs and gifts from the atomic era.

GO BACK TO THE FUTURE
AT THE HOOVER DAM

The Hoover Dam and Boulder City are remarkable symbols of human innovation, harnessing the power of nature for the greater good. Boulder City, a place of hope and prosperity, was founded in 1931, emerging from the desert as a housing community for the workers building the dam. The Hoover Dam, an engineering marvel, has significant environmental benefits and is critical to the American Southwest's ecosystem, demonstrating that conservation and development coexist. The dam's architectural design and art deco elements, set against the breathtaking beauty of Boulder City, Lake Mead, and the surrounding mountainous landscapes, provide a compelling reason to visit!

Hoover Dam
usbr.gov/lc/hooverdam

Boulder City
bcnv.org

TIP

Boulder City is a charming community with small-town comforts like diners, lodges, and motels. It has a thoughtful appeal of yesteryear. While you're at the Hoover Dam, and just for the nostalgia, take a unique thrill-hop an hour into the past. Then, in mere seconds, return back to the future! The dam is located on the border of Arizona and Nevada, making it possible to straddle time.

VIEW THE WORLD'S LARGEST
CHOCOLATE FOUNTAIN

The Bellagio features more than one world-renowned fountain. Inside the resort is the Bellagio Chocolate Fountain, adding to the grandeur of Las Vegas attractions. However, this indoor fountain does not spray water. Instead, it combines gourmet chocolate with architectural genius, creating a luxurious infinite flow of chocolate in a stunning fluted-glass casing. Guinness World Records says this is the world's largest chocolate fountain. Therefore, you can expect to be captivated by its grandeur and mesmerizing flow of three kinds of melted sweets. White, dark, and milk chocolates make it a work of culinary art. Its Instagramable nature makes it a Vegas must-visit!

3600 Las Vegas Blvd. S, 702-693-8865
bellagio.mgmresorts.com/en/restaurants/bellagio-patisserie.html

---

TIP

When visiting the world-record chocolate fountain, take a moment to enjoy a quick snack at the Bellagio Patisserie. This cozy French café features the charming chocolate fountain, and it offers a delectable selection of pastries, snacks, salads, and sandwiches for a quick and delightful bite at any time of the day.

UNCOVER WHAT'S THE DEAL
WITH OMEGA MART

Meow Wolf Las Vegas is an interactive surrealist attraction just a mile west of the Strip. The highlight inside Meow Wolf is its Omega Mart, an extraordinary supermarket that doubles as an art installation. This unique experience features real-fake grocery products and artistic displays created by hundreds of artists worldwide, making it a playful museum and a celebration of creativity and imagination.

But that's not all! Beyond the mart, through various strange passageways, such as walking through a grocery store freezer, lies a hidden dimension. It's a realm of trippy psychedelic colors, vibrant light displays, secret portals, and unexpected landscapes that will surprise and delight you. Meow Wolf Las Vegas is an immersive destination that promises a thrilling journey of surprises and excitement at every turn!

3215 S Rancho Dr., #100 Las Vegas, 866-636-9969
meowwolf.com/visit/las-vegas

TIE THE KNOT IN LAS VEGAS
OR WITNESS A WEDDING

Las Vegas has long been a premier destination for couples looking to tie the knot. Since 1953, the city has been officially known as the "Marriage Capital of the World." With the help of Elvis, Vegas marries more couples than any other destination worldwide. This is primarily due to the ease of acquiring a marriage license, the minimal costs of having a wedding here, and the city's advantage of all-year picturesque weather, ensuring a beautiful backdrop for your special day. Whether it's a celebrity private wedding, an elopement, or a thoughtfully planned destination wedding, Vegas is the place that makes any season the best time to get married!

Not getting married? A neat thing to do is visit "Wedding Row" in Downtown Las Vegas, which celebrates the city's thriving wedding industry. It rings together several of Vegas's 60-plus chapels and the Clark County Marriage License Bureau.

For more information, visit:
weddings.vegas

TIP

Vegas's nuptial options include same-day weddings, chapel wedding packages, and even drive-through weddings. You may have heard of the world-famous drive-up "Tunnel of Love Ceremony" at the Little White Wedding Chapel, where many celebrities walked down the aisle, including Michael Jordan, Britney Spears, and J.Lo!

1301 S Las Vegas Blvd., 702-382-5943
alittlewhitechapel.com

Or opt for a nostalgic ceremony at the oldest wedding chapel in Las Vegas, the Graceland Wedding Chapel. Established in 1939, it gained recognition as the first chapel in the world to host an Elvis-themed wedding ceremony in 1977.

619 Las Vegas Blvd. S, 702-382-0091
gracelandchapel.com

SNAP A PHOTO
WITH VEGAS'S ICONIC COUPLE

A trip to Downtown Las Vegas wouldn't be complete without delving into its storied past. So, take a photo with Fremont Street's unofficial welcoming signs, Vegas Vic and Vegas Vickie, which are must-sees for anyone interested in the city's history. Vegas Vic, a massive neon-lit sign, was erected in 1951 on the exterior of the now-retired casino the Pioneer Club. Vic was a departure from traditional typeface signs, featuring a friendly cowboy figure. Similarly, Vegas Vickie, a neon sign of a cowgirl in a fringed outfit, arrived in Downtown Las Vegas in 1980 and originally stood atop the Girls of Glitter Gulch. Both signs have been restored and can still be seen at the Fremont Street Experience.

TIP

Fun fact: True to "What Happens in Vegas," Vegas Vic and Vegas Vickie were "married" in 1994 during the construction of the Fremont Street Experience! Vic remains outside a souvenir shop on Fremont Street, which used to be the Pioneer Club. His wife, Vickie, is just across the way inside Circa Resort & Casino, the property that replaced the Girls of Glitter Gulch where her story began.

UNCOVER THE UNIQUE CHARM
OF THE LAS VEGAS FARM

Come experience the joy of connecting with nature at the Las Vegas Farm. For over 50 years, the nonprofit animal rescue and eco-friendly farm has been a hub for community engagement and agricultural education. It has timelessly welcomed visitors, providing a sanctuary for farm animals, large and small, including peacocks, pigs, cows, horses, chickens, turtles, goats, alpacas, llamas, and hundreds of roaming cats!

You can visit the Las Vegas Farm every weekend (Saturday to Sunday) during the day and enjoy seasonal events and special festivities. An affordable entry fee supports the animal friends. Visitors can also purchase feed to interact with the animals. There's no entry fee to browse the farm's inviting and rustic marketplace, which features fresh produce grown on-site, eggs, and locally sourced honey. You can also purchase locally produced jams, pies, bread, butter, and seasonal goods, providing a delightful reminder of the benefits of sustainable farming and the beautiful connection between nature, animals, and humans.

7222 W Grand Teton Dr., 702-982-8000
thelasvegasfarm.com

SUPPORT DIVERSE COMMUNITIES
AT A CULTURAL FESTIVAL

Las Vegas festivals showcase cultural vibrancy with a spirit of unity, belonging, and sheer fun! Notable festivals in the city include the Flavors of Aloha Hawaii Festival, the annual Las Vegas Juneteenth Festival, the Rumbazo Latin Music Festival, the Filipino Pinoy Pride Festival, and the Las Vegas PRIDE Festival, which features a lively parade—the largest in the state! All of these festivals share a common thread of community engagement.

If you're a food and drink enthusiast, rejoice because Las Vegas festivals offer a wide range of local and international cuisine, from savory to sweet. Live music, performed in Vegas entertainment style, fills the air while artisans and craft makers display their talents at various stalls, promoting support for local talent. Note that except for Flavors of Aloha and the annual Juneteenth Festival, these cultural celebrations usually occur in the fall, when the weather in Vegas is comfortable day and night.

Flavors of Aloha
flavorsofaloha.com

Rumbazo Music Festival
rumbazofest.com

Las Vegas Juneteenth Festival
june19lv.com

Pinoy Pride Festival
darnaevents.com

Las Vegas PRIDE Festival
lasvegaspride.org

COSPLAY AT LAS VEGAS COMIC CON

Every year, Las Vegas hosts a unique event that brings together fans of fantasy fiction, superhero movies, and more—Amazing Las Vegas Comic Con. It's an extraordinary fan experience and so much more than just another convention. The cosplay community at Comic Con showcases boundless creativity and unyielding passion. From beginners who blossom to experts who astonish with their elaborate costume creations, the atmosphere is electric.

The real thrill is seeing your favorite artists and celebrities up close. This unique opportunity and learning behind-the-scenes tidbits of the series you adore make Comic Con an inclusive and memorable fan experience. And bonus, it's in Vegas, baby!

amazingcomiccon.com/amazing-las-vegas

TIP

One destination to plan for is the Millennium FANDOM BAR, the ultimate Vegas hangout and bar for everything Comic Con geek and fandom culture, from themed cocktails to cosplay events!

900 S Las Vegas Blvd., #140, 702-405-0816, fandombar.com

GLOBE-TROT
IN LAS VEGAS

Las Vegas is a gateway to adventures around the world without the need for a flight. Here, you'll discover inspiring attractions that transport you around the globe in mere minutes! Visit the Eiffel Tower's observation deck at Paris Las Vegas, with sweeping views of the city skyline. Enjoy gondola rides that evoke the charm of winding Venetian canals just before exploring architectural wonders at Caesars Palace that mimic the columns of ancient Rome. Wander to Egypt to see the sphinx and pyramid at the Luxor before ending your trip at the edge of the Las Vegas Strip. There, you'll discover the beautiful sandy beaches of Mandalay Bay, reminiscent of the tropical islands of the Philippines.

Vegas has cleverly curated a treasure trove of world-renowned sites, including America's iconic New York-New York *Statue of Liberty*, and Toshiba Plaza that mimics the ambiance of Manhattan's Central Park. It's one of the few cities where you can see legendary landmarks from various countries without leaving the boulevard.

TIP

Las Vegas is also a global culinary hub with diverse food experiences from Asian to European cuisines. Luxury dining destinations, certified by Forbes Travel Guide, enhance the city's international appeal. Experiencing the world's flavors is possible here without needing to travel abroad!

SIGHTSEE ON A BIG BUS TOUR

Big Bus Tours are renowned for their unique Las Vegas sightseeing experiences that provide the perfect introduction to the city. These adventures showcase must-see landmarks in Las Vegas, from Downtown "Old Vegas" to the dazzling casinos and resorts of the Strip. You can choose to sightsee from an open-top bus or the lower level inside. Wherever you choose to sit, the tour offers audio guides, stunning city views, and the perfect setting for the best photos and videos.

With options like the Las Vegas Discover Ticket, the Essential Ticket, and the Night Tours you're likely to rave about, the flexibility to explore at your own pace is at your fingertips. These personalized tour packages allow you to hop off at fascinating Vegas landmarks and hop back on when you're ready for more!

bigbustours.com

HAVE A BLAST
IN CHINATOWN

Chinatown Vegas is a fascinating three-mile neighborhood district a few blocks from the Las Vegas Strip. It offers a rich cultural experience through its diverse shopping, entertainment, and, of course, delicious food! Chinatown is a shopper's paradise, with more than 150 restaurants, 40 spas, six Asian supermarkets, 12 churches, and more! Day and night, it's a hive of activity, with tourists and locals flocking to its best restaurants and shops. When you've had your fill of shopping and dining, you can explore attractions like Floyd Mayweather Jr.'s gym, enjoy foot reflexology, showcase your singing skills at a karaoke joint, or blow off some steam at a wreck room.

chinatownvegas.com

TIP

Parking in this area can be challenging. To make the most of your Chinatown adventure, consider using rideshare services to avoid the stress of finding a parking spot and focus on having a great time instead!

CELEBRATE
THE BLACK COMMUNITY'S CONTRIBUTIONS TO LAS VEGAS

Explore the Historic Westside district in Las Vegas, known for its rich Black history and culture. As Las Vegas became the Entertainment Capital of the World in the 1950s and 1960s, the African American community in the Westside played a pivotal role in the city's growth, taking on jobs often inaccessible to Black individuals elsewhere in the country.

The Westside's Black community fueled the city's entertainment scene and contributed significantly to its identity. The area around Jackson Avenue flourished with the opening of the Moulin Rouge Hotel, the first fully integrated casino in the city. The Moulin Rouge tragically fell victim to an arson fire in 2003, but its legacy lives on as a part of the National Register of Historic Places.

Today, the Historic Westside boasts a variety of Black-owned restaurants, cafés, theaters, and cultural landmarks, including the West Las Vegas Arts Center, the Historic Westside Murals Project, the Historic Westside Legacy Park, Harrison House, and the *Martin Luther King Jr.* statue. Vegas's Historic Westside is a destination worth visiting any day, where you'll witness the thriving future of the new generation while honoring its rich history.

Located northwest of the Las Vegas Strip
and the "Spaghetti Bowl" interchange of I-15 and I-11/US 95.
visitlasvegas.com/historicwestside

DISCOVER THE ENCHANTMENT
OF LAS VEGAS LIVING

You can discover a different side of Las Vegas by going on a celebrity or luxury home tour. This unique experience grants access to the lavish current and former homes of some of the city's most beloved entertainers who helped define the city's allure. The enchantment begins as you're chauffeured into the worlds of Michael Jackson, Liberace, Gladys Knight, Wayne Newton, Siegfried & Roy, and more!

Because Vegas isn't only an entertainment playground, it's home to nearly 3 million residents and has one of the country's most compelling and prosperous real estate stories. It might be surprising to learn that most Vegas locals don't live on or near the Strip. Still, it's Vegas, so the extraordinary becomes the norm. This is probably why many residents choose this city for its scenic master-planned communities, which make it feel like you're living in a resort! And as a bonus, Nevada is home to some of the lowest property tax rates in the US, making homes here easier to afford.

The Celebrity Homes Tour
702-827-4101
anothersideoflasvegastours.com

Vegas Luxury Home Tours
702-417-7839
vegasluxuryhometours.com

TIP

When visiting Las Vegas, consider exploring beyond the Strip and heading north toward Red Rock Canyon and the suburbs of Summerlin to the west. This community is known for its high-end amenities and guarded gated entries. Still, it offers a peaceful and serene side of Las Vegas that most tourists rarely get to know. It's a breathtaking escape through dream neighborhoods and exquisite communities waiting for you to explore!

summerlin.com

Fashion Show Las Vegas

SHOPPING AND FASHION

SHOP
AT A FARMERS MARKET

Look behind the scenes into the Las Vegas locals' hidden guide of best-kept secrets, and you'll stumble upon our bustling farmers markets. Envision a Vegas-style spectacle of colossal, bright, colorful fruits and vegetables. These markets embody the spirit and wholesomeness in Sin City, hosting thrilling pop-up events where locals, often accompanied by their furry friends, gather to purchase the freshest flowers and organic produce. Vegas farmers markets are a haven of talented specialty vendors, offering everything from handmade candles to artisan jewelry, sustainable clothing, and more. Each visit offers you an exciting and varied experience. Visit each market's website to find current times and locations.

Las Vegas Farmers Market
1980 Festival Plaza Dr.
summerlin.com/event/
las-vegas-farmers-market

Fresh52 Farmers & Artisan
Markets
fresh52.com

TIP

Vintage Market Days is an upscale outdoor market held twice a year in the spring and fall. It features original art, antiques, clothing, jewelry, home decor, outdoor furnishings, delicious treats, and much more!

Downtown Summerlin, 1825 Festival Plaza Dr.
vintagemarketdays.com/market/southern-nevada

HANDPICK PRODUCE FROM THE FIELD
AT GILCREASE ORCHARD

Gilcrease Orchard offers a truly unique farm-to-table experience, allowing you to handpick your own produce straight from the field. Just a short drive from the Las Vegas Strip, this hidden gem was established to provide fresh, locally sourced produce and promote sustainable agriculture and local farming. The farm, which started with over 900 acres by Mrs. Gilcrease and her sons, now harvests the freshest apples, peaches, pomegranates, pears, sunflowers, and more. There's also an on-site restaurant for breakfast and lunch featuring live musicians, adding an exclusive touch to your visit.

As autumn arrives, the landscape transforms into an inviting festival where you can enjoy fall harvest activities. These include pumpkin patch picking, cutting sunflowers from the fields, wagon rides, a corn maze, a hay maze, and apple and pear cider drinks. Gilcrease's seasonal apple cider doughnuts are a standout treat and rival the deliciousness of beloved Krispy Kreme!

Discovering this peaceful countryside haven in Las Vegas's lit-up landscape may be surprising. But Gilcrease Orchard offers a distinctive farm-to-table experience, serving as a vital link to nature and agritourism in Vegas.

7800 N Tenaya Way, 702-409-0655
thegilcreaseorchard.org

SEARCH FOR RARE FINDS
AT GOLD & SILVER PAWN SHOP

There will be pawn shops where there are casinos, and Las Vegas is a city synonymous with casinos! Among the 60-plus pawn shops in the Vegas Valley, one stands out—Gold & Silver Pawn Shop. Here, you can browse, sell, or shop for rare finds. But what truly sets this place apart is its direct link to the popular reality show *Pawn Stars*, a fact that excites many tourists. But do the *Pawn Stars* guys actually work in the store?

Spoiler alert! They do not. However, the pawn shop featured in the series is a real-life, fully functional store on Las Vegas Boulevard. The producers created a "duplicate store" for filming. The replica store is an exact match, allowing the actual store's business to operate smoothly without interruption.

713 S Las Vegas Blvd., 702-385-7912
gspawn.com

TIP

Pawn Plaza, located in Downtown Las Vegas, is a retail district owned by the show's star, Rick Harrison. It's next door to the world-famous Gold & Silver Pawn Shop, creating a unique synergy between the two locations. Pawn Plaza might be the best place to have a chance to see the cast of *Pawn Stars*, as it's home to restaurants, retail stores, and the cast's other businesses. Rick owns Rick's Rollin' Smoke BBQ, where he's been seen bartending, and Chumlee Russell has Chumlee's Candy inside Pawn Plaza.

EXPERIENCE FLEA MARKET SHOPPING
AND MARIACHI BAND MUSIC

Broadacres Marketplace is a vibrant destination in North Las Vegas, celebrated for its diverse offerings. From food to local produce, entertainment, carnival rides, and unique shopping options, there's something for everyone at this lively location. This expansive outdoor flea market, open only on the weekends, celebrates Mexican culture and mariachi band music. You're guaranteed to get more than you bargained for and leave with a festival experience!

Local artisans and merchants gather at Broadacres Marketplace, setting up shop under tented vendor booths surrounding a large center stage with ample covered tables and seating. But this lively hub is more than just a marketplace. It's a fantastic opportunity to support and appreciate the talents of local performers while exploring the diverse Las Vegas market.

2930 Las Vegas Blvd. N, North Las Vegas, 702-642-3777
broadacresm.com

For indoor Vegas flea market shops, check out:
Fantastic Indoor Swap Meet
1717 S Decatur Blcd., 702-877-0087
fantasticindoorswapmeet.com

TREASURE HUNT
AT ANTIQUE ALLEY

Venturing down Antique Alley, a row of vintage and antique shops in Downtown Las Vegas, you'll discover an eclectic treasure trove of finds from old Vegas hotel memorabilia to quirky store signs like "Vintage Vegas: Dead People's Junk & Cool Crap." The vibrant Bohemian boutiques blend Las Vegas history with a modern-day treasure-hunting experience. One notable spot to visit is the Antique Alley Mall, home to boutique shops and vendor stalls offering retro clothing, home decor, antiques, kitschy collectibles, and unique oddities that resonate with the vintage charm of Vegas and eras gone by.

1126 S Main St., 702-684-5177
antiquealleymall.com

TIP

Patience isn't just a virtue but a crucial tool for exploring the paths of Antique Alley Mall. Countless rows of vendor booths and unique finds whisper stories of yesteryear. To keep it interesting, engage with the local business owners while exploring the various shops. Remember, unlocking the secrets of the alley requires patience to let the history of Las Vegas reveal itself to you!

DISCOVER ANTIQUES

A few miles beyond Antique Alley lies Downtown Container Park, an unconventional open-air shopping center constructed from shipping containers!

707 E Fremont St., 702-359-9982
downtowncontainerpark.com

Closer to the Las Vegas Strip is Bonanza Gift Shop, the "World's Largest Gift Shop" with over 40,000 square feet of dedicated retail space. It has Las Vegas souvenirs, apparel deals, whimsical items, kids' toys, novelties, Vegas gag gifts, and more! It also boasts the largest liquor selection on the Strip.

2400 S Las Vegas Blvd., 702-385-7359
bonanza-gift-shop.weeblyte.com

GET THRIFTY IN VEGAS

Discovering the thrifting scene in Las Vegas goes beyond just another hunt for great deals. It's about finding treasures with a story, turning someone else's unwanted items into your new favorite finds! Whether browsing a vintage boutique or a thrift store, you'll feel the history of past decades blending with present possibilities. From everyday clothing to unique Vegas show props like showgirl costumes, leather chaps, or sparkly platform shoes, there's a thrill in discovering items that reflect the vibrant culture of Las Vegas.

Still, thrifting is primarily about making smart shopping decisions and getting more value for your money. Thrift stores in Las Vegas offer the chance to snag branded goods, ones you've eyed for months, at a fraction of their original prices, providing an eco-friendly way to shop by giving items a second life.

TIP

Big brand thrift stores in Vegas, like Goodwill, Habitat for Humanity, and Savers, offer a variety of items, and they usually organize them well. Unique thrift stores such as Buffalo Exchange, Alt Rebel, and Glam Factory Vintage provide a more curated selection if you're seeking one-of-a-kind finds. Proceeds from Las Vegas thrift stores often go toward supporting good causes, like the only-in-Vegas thrift store Dog Junkies.

Buffalo Exchange
1209 S Main St., 702-791-3960
buffaloexchange.com/location/arts-district-las-vegas

Alt Rebel
1409 S Commerce St., Ste. 110, 702-522-9037
shopaltrebel.com

Glam Factory Vintage
211 E Colorado Ave., 702-443-0131
instagram.com/glam_factory

Dog Junkies Thrift Store
4324 N Decatur Blvd., 702-778-2558
ahome4spot.com/dogjunkies

VISIT THE WORLD MARKET CENTER

The World Market Center Las Vegas is an international epicenter for interior designers, buyers, and retailers. Luxury resorts in Vegas depend on this center to acquire unique and custom interior selections, including furniture, fixtures, decor, gift shop items, and displays. With 5.3 million square feet across three buildings and three pavilions on a 57-acre site, this place is a global headquarters for unique, custom, and designer pieces.

The center hosts the colossal Las Vegas Market trade show, allowing apparel, home furnishings, gift, design, and manufacturing industry members to discover the latest decor and seasonal items. Inside is a must-see-to-believe showcase of thousands of gorgeous glass-encased exhibitor showrooms spanning over 40 floors of its combined buildings!

475 S Grand Central Pkwy., 702-599-9621
wmclv.com

TIP

Twice a year, usually in the spring and fall, the World Market Center Las Vegas opens its doors to the public for a huge sample sale! You can shop sample boutique pieces for a fraction of the wholesale cost. Otherwise, Building A on the World Market Center campus, also known as the Las Vegas Design Center, is always open to the public for browsing on the first two floors.

SEE THE PRODUCTS OF THE FUTURE
BEFORE ANYONE ELSE

Get ready for the future of tech at CES (formerly the Consumer Electronics Show). Every year, CES takes over Las Vegas, unveiling the world's cutting-edge innovations. With satellite locations and showrooms along the Vegas Strip, this massive event showcases the latest tech creations with a unique opportunity to interact with and meet the masterminds behind them. From autonomous vehicles, robots, and AI assistants to smart homes, TVs, and more, CES is the world showcase and global stage for tomorrow's boldest breakthroughs and groundbreaking technology!

Las Vegas Convention Center
3150 Paradise Rd.
ces.tech

TIP

If you're a tech industry member, you can register to attend CES and buy conference tickets on the website. If you're a member of the media, you can get exclusive early access passes to experience everything before anyone else! If you're an interested consumer, check out your favorite Las Vegas influencers for live streams of the inside scoop at CES.

SHOP HIGH-END DESIGNER STORES
ON THE LAS VEGAS STRIP

Vegas is the ultimate luxury shopping destination, offering many designer options that will surely excite your inner big spender! Its top-tier destinations provide a high-end touch and convenient experience. The famous Strip is lined with luxury stores, all conveniently situated inside the shopping malls of the renowned resorts. Whether you're looking for mid-level stores like Nike or high-end brands like Gucci, you'll find it all here, making your shopping experience a breeze.

At the Forum Shops at Caesars, you can shop at world-renowned destinations such as Tiffany & Co., Christian Louboutin, and Versace, all housed in a stunning Roman-themed mall. The contemporary Shops at Crystals is the only all-luxury shopping destination in the country that brings together the world's most elite, high fashion brands. Its unique architectural design and striking crystalline structure set it apart from other malls. Interestingly, these branded stores are positioned for an upscale marketing strategy rather than solely focusing on retail revenue generated by sales.

Another shopping complex in Las Vegas is Downtown Summerlin, in the suburbs off the Strip. Shopaholics are drawn to this modern outdoor mall by its picturesque landscape, which resembles an opulent lifestyle backdrop made for TV.

EXTRAVAGANT MALLS AND BOUTIQUE STORES

The Forum Shops at Caesars Palace
3500 Las Vegas Blvd. S, 702-893-4800
simon.com/mall/the-forum-shops-at-caesars-palace

Fashion Show Las Vegas
3200 Las Vegas Blvd. S, Ste. 600, 702-784-7000
fslv.com

The Shops at Crystals
3720 S Las Vegas Blvd., 702-590-9299
simon.com/mall/the-shops-at-crystals

Tivoli Village
400 S Rampart Blvd., 702-534-0000
tivolivillagelv.com

Downtown Summerlin
1980 Festival Plaza Dr., 702-832-1000
summerlin.com/downtown-summerlin

Looking for luxury deals? Make a short trip
north or south of the Strip to the Las Vegas
Premium Outlets.

Las Vegas North Premium Outlets
875 S Grand Central Pkwy., 702-474-7500
premiumoutlets.com/outlet/las-vegas-north

Las Vegas South Premium Outlets
7400 Las Vegas Blvd. S, 702-896-5599
premiumoutlets.com/outlet/las-vegas-south

TREAT YOURSELF
TO A LUXURIOUS SPA EXPERIENCE

Treat yourself to a luxurious spa experience in Las Vegas! There are multiple five-star spas on the Strip within the famed resorts. However, Fontainebleau's Lapis Spa & Wellness is a standout choice. Enjoy hours of access to wellness experiences including the Stargazing Lounge, pools, steam room, infrared sauna, Himalayan salt room, salt mist therapy, oxygen therapy, heated spa loungers, and cold-plunge pools. The Star & Snow Showers is a fantasy-like feature where delicate snow flurries are released for a lavish cooldown after a heated treatment. This hot-cold therapy also includes a heated floor to keep your feet warm and melt the snow as it lands!

In Downtown Las Vegas, the Golden Nugget has one of the few spa retreats at the Fremont Street Experience. Choose a day pass or individual services and indulgences, including a whirlpool, steam room, hot plunge, chakra balances, facials, body scrubs, and massages. One unique feature is the Reset Suite, which has a zero-gravity lounge chair, guided meditation headphones, and heated eye massage masks.

Lapis Spa & Wellness at Fontainebleau
2777 S Las Vegas Blvd., 833-702-7878
fontainebleaulasvegas.com/wellness/lapis-spa-and-wellness/

Spa & Salon at the Golden Nugget
129 Fremont St., 702-386-8186
goldennugget.com/las-vegas/amenities/spa-salon

TIP

Additionally, most Vegas spas offer waxing, nail services, hair styling, and professional makeup applications, ensuring you leave feeling relaxed and ready for a night out on the town.

If you want a unique spa experience in suburban Las Vegas, check out Spring Valley's Desert Beauty Lab. This spa offers customizable pedicures with amenities such as hot tea, pillows, blankets, and treatments like hot stone therapy, chakra balancing, and sound baths. At the same time, you relax in a reclining zero-gravity chair.

7260 S Cimarron Rd., Ste. 110, 702-640-0100
desertbeautylab.com

ACTIVITIES
BY SEASON

WINTER

SPRING

SUMMER

FALL

• •

SUGGESTED
ITINERARIES

CULTURAL CONNECTIONS

DATE NIGHT

FAMILY FRIENDLY FUN

OUTDOOR ADVENTURES

• •

HOLIDAY SPIRIT

INDEX

• •